NEVER
LOSE
AGAIN

—►◄—

NEVER LOSE AGAIN

Become a Top Negotiator
by Asking the Right Questions

Steven Babitsky and James J. Mangraviti Jr.

THOMAS DUNNE BOOKS
St. Martin's Press   **New York**

THOMAS DUNNE BOOKS.
An imprint of St. Martin's Press.

NEVER LOSE AGAIN. Copyright © 2011 by Steven Babitsky and James J. Mangraviti Jr. All rights reserved. Printed in the United States of America. For information, address St. Martin's Press, 175 Fifth Avenue, New York, N.Y. 10010.

www.thomasdunnebooks.com
www.stmartins.com

Book design by Sarah Maya Gubkin

Library of Congress Cataloging-in-Publication Data

Babitsky, Steven.
    Never lose again : become a top negotiator by asking the right questions /
Steven Babitsky and James J. Mangraviti Jr.
        p. cm.
    ISBN 978-0-312-64348-5 (alk. paper)
    1. Negotiation in business.   I. Mangraviti, James.   II. Title.
    HD58.6.B34 2011
    658.4'052—dc22

                                                            2010037512

First Edition: January 2011

10 9 8 7 6 5 4 3 2 1

To Alex, Karen, Jimmy, and Katie

CONTENTS

ACKNOWLEDGMENTS

Billy and Peter, you each made this book far better than we ever could have made it without your help. We are deeply grateful.

INTRODUCTION

Larry, a twenty-four-year-old apprentice electrician and Vietnam veteran, was working on a triple-decker house in Boston, Massachusetts, installing outside lighting. He leaned back against a railing that cracked, sending him falling backward. He hit a clothesline on his way down and broke his neck. Larry was taken to the hospital, underwent surgery, and was told several days later that he was permanently paralyzed from the shoulders down and was a quadriplegic. After his hospital stay, the workers' compensation insurance company, which was responsible for his care, moved him to a one-bedroom handicapped apartment in an elderly housing unit. The insurance company paid his twenty-three-year-old wife $150 a week to take care of him twenty-four hours a day. His wife became exhausted and desperate. After a year she divorced him and married his best friend. Larry was now left alone, with sporadic care, and was deteriorating physically and mentally.

Larry contacted a law office and asked for help. A young lawyer went to his house and met him. He was so upset about Larry's condition and situation that he was unable to return to his law office that day. The young attorney actually felt physically ill.

The fresh-out-of-law-school lawyer represented Larry for three years, helping him pursue his workers' compensation claim against the insurance company. During these years he was able to negotiate for a handicapped van, an accessible home, twenty-four-hour health care, and eventually a generous settlement that provided him with lifetime security. Larry was able to move to a warmer climate, Southern California. His full-time nurse moved with him, and he has been healthy and happy for the past thirty-five years. He remains a good friend of the lawyer to this day.

At the conclusion of the negotiated settlement with the workers' compensation insurance company, Larry asked his lawyer to come close to him in his wheelchair and whispered in his ear, "Steve, you saved my life."

The young lawyer in this story is one of this book's authors, Steve Babitsky. It was at this time that Steve realized for the first time the power of effective negotiating, and how much of a difference it can and does make in the lives of the people it touches. This experience ignited a passion in Steve for developing negotiating skills, and teaching those skills to others.

A young lawyer from Steve's alma mater, Boston College Law School, joined his training firm in 1993. His name is Jim Mangraviti and he became Steve's protégé and coauthor on numerous books, including this one.

Together we run our nationally renowned training and consulting firm, SEAK, Inc. Many of the examples and stories in this book come directly from or are inspired by our business dealings over the years.

This book is intended to empower the reader to markedly improve his or her life through effective negotiating. Our aim is to change the way people think about and approach negotiations. Many people dread negotiating. Many are just poor negotiators. We make better negotiation results simple and easy to achieve. Negotiating is a fact of life and is essential for obtaining what you and your family deserve. Avoiding negotiation is not an option. It's a necessary part of daily life, from your phone bill to your professional dealings at work. The only choices are: learn to thrive and succeed or suffer the consequences. This book will teach the reader how to be a much better negotiator.

About ten years ago, a shocking negotiation episode we both witnessed first-hand finally pushed us to act to help our clients become better negotiators.

We were in Hawaii teaching a training course for physicians that our company was putting on. With us was a young primary care physician who was neither a high-earner nor wealthy; he was a father of four, living paycheck to paycheck (we'll call him Ted). His dream was to someday retire to Hawaii. At lunch Ted asked us to take a look with him at a condominium that was for sale nearby.

We had one hour for lunch, so we and Ted drove over to the condominium complex to look at a two-bedroom unit. The listing agent for the condo was present, and Ted went on and on to her about how he loved the unit, how he knew it would go up in price, and how his dream was to retire to Hawaii. The (by-then salivating) agent informed Ted that this was the only unit of its type left, a couple was coming to put a down payment on this particular unit in a few hours, and the price was $250,000.

The shocking "negotiation" we witnessed consisted of the following:

Ted: "I really want this. Can I negotiate the price?"

Realtor: "No."

Ted then called his wife and asked her how much money they had in their emergency checking account. He then asked her to FedEx their checkbook. He proceeded to sign dozens of pages of documents provided by the agent in blank (they didn't even specify what unit he was buying or the price), without reading them, and purchased the unit at the full asking price, all within thirty-five minutes.

The three of us returned to the seminar. We couldn't believe what we had just witnessed. We were stunned. How could a person as intelligent as a physician be such a terrible negotiator? How could he be so gullible as to fall for the line about a couple coming back with a deposit? How could he be so reckless as to sign numerous legal documents in blank without even reading them himself, never mind having a lawyer review them. Anybody who knew even basic negotiation skills such as not showing your hand, generating power, *and asking the right questions,* might have been able to save tens of thousands of dollars on this purchase. After we got back to the training session, Ted told his story about how he had just purchased the condo over the lunch break, and immediately two or three other physician colleagues in the seminar went over to see if there were any units available for them!

This was the moment when we both realized that there was a desperate need for even highly educated people to learn how to negotiate. This realization is confirmed time and again by recent events. One need not look any further than the botched attempt by Jerry Yang to sell Yahoo to Microsoft in 2008. His clumsy strategy and attempt to sell his company is the classic example of a failed negotiation and what can go wrong when you do not understand how to negotiate. In May 2008, Yahoo CEO Jerry Yang was offered $45.7 billion by Microsoft CEO Steve Ballmer to acquire Yahoo. This was rejected by Mr. Yang, who was holding out for $55 billion. After months of rejections by Yang, Mr. Ballmer had enough and completely withdrew his $50 billion. This failed negotiation cost Mr. Yang his job and resulted in a loss to Yahoo of approximately $20 billion. We see it all the time in the news, with high-profile mergers like the Yahoo one, but negotiation, no matter how big or small, is part of everyone's everyday life as well.

After the Hawaii condo incident described above we decided to act. We soon added in-person negotiation training to SEAK's lineup of seminars and consulting services. Our negotiation training was delivered through continuing education seminars, in-house corporate training, and one-on-one negotiation consulting. We also coauthored two successful books, which SEAK published, on how physicians can become better negotiators.

The concept for this book evolved out of our training of thousands of professionals across the United States. During this training we learned two main things:

- **Many highly intelligent people are not good negotiators.**

- **People who are good negotiators do much better financially, professionally, and have a better lifestyle.**

Negotiating is an art. It is complicated. To become an exceptional negotiator traditionally requires years of practice, but that doesn't mean that most people couldn't quickly and easily learn good negotiating practices if someone shows them what to do. This book does exactly that. We have made improved negotiating skills easy to learn and easy to implement. The book distills our twenty-plus years of experience in negotiating training into 50 questions that anyone can quickly learn and use immediately.

Our unique concept is to give the reader the secrets to quickly and easily become a far better negotiator. That's the essence of our book—negotiation advice that is quick and easy to learn, and yet remarkably effective since the reader can easily apply the advice by asking the suggested questions in the appropriate negotiation scenario. Best of all, our questions apply to all types of negotiation situations, from buying a home or an automobile, to business transactions of all kinds, and even to getting better rates from phone and cable companies. Often, more than one of the questions can be used over the course of a negotiation.

Each time we teach our negotiation classes, we invariably are asked by our attendees for a list of the best questions to ask. This is the takeaway that is most desired and valued. The reason for this is simple and compelling: Knowing the best questions to ask makes you a better negotiator immediately.

When we travel the country and teach people how to negotiate effectively, our attendees undergo a metamorphosis. At first, they are skeptical, but once we demonstrate the effectiveness of the negotiation questions we provide for them, they quickly see how they can make those questions work for them. It is like going to the optometrist for new glasses. The optometrist first puts in the lenses that aren't strong enough, so your vision's still blurry. He then puts in lenses that grow stronger progressively until you smile and see perfectly. This is how the attendees react to the questions and training. The blurriness is removed, and they see the negotiating lessons perfectly.

Our negotiation questions work. We use them ourselves all the time. In fact, we really knew we were onto something when we began pitching this book idea to editors, and the editors told us that they had tried out and were successfully using our questions themselves.

We have designed this book to be very easy to use and quick to read. Each question is set out in separate two- to three-page chapters. In addition, each chapter contains a quick summary "lesson."

We have also added a section in each chapter that contains possible responses in case *you* are asked the question during the course of a negotiation. These sample answers are just a guide, of course. How you should respond to a question depends upon the precise situation and negotiations you are facing.

The points we would like you to take from the sample answers are as follows. First, if you are well prepared, even very difficult questions can oftentimes have effective answers—sometimes extremely effective answers. Second, there is not a perfect answer to every negotiation question; sometimes there's not even a good answer to a tough question. Third, you almost always have the option of either dodging the question or just answering a different question—never feel as though you are required to answer a question in the precise way the other party hoped you would answer it. This last point is often one of the hardest to practice by new negotiators who somehow might think it rude or inappropriate not to cooperate with the other party. Sophisticated negotiators come to realize that there is usually nothing wrong with not answering many negotiating questions the way the other party intended you to. It happens all the time.

The final reason we have included sample answers is that these serve to further teach the reader about the negotiating process in general. When we provide our analysis for why a certain response may be a good one we also provide a good deal of commentary on negotiation strategy, tactics, and concepts. We felt that this additional commentary, in the context of specific questions and answers, is a quick and easy way to improve the reader's overall appreciation of the many complex and dynamic subtleties and nuances of a negotiation.

We have organized the questions loosely in ten categories, or parts, and included a brief introduction to each part. The purpose of these introductions is to provide concise negotiating theory and help the reader to connect the dots.

There is no question in our minds that those who can best negotiate will be best positioned to succeed. It is our earnest hope that our book will empower the reader to immediately and vastly improve their negotiation skills, and succeed in business and life.

PART I

Stealth Information Gathering

INTRODUCTION: Success in negotiation is often directly related to how much accurate information you can gather concerning the other party's goals, deadlines, and alternatives. For example, if you were able to determine that the other party was under a tight deadline and didn't know where else to turn, you would be in an extremely favorable negotiating position. A highly effective way to gather useful information is through the seemingly innocuous questions detailed below that are designed to get the other party to reveal valuable information.

Question #1

HOW DID YOU HEAR ABOUT US?

Information translates directly into negotiating power. The more information you have when negotiating, the better off you will be. "How did you hear about us?" is a superb, zero-risk question that should be used routinely by sellers in an attempt to gather information.

The idea behind "How did you hear about us?" is simply to get the potential buyer talking. The question itself is very open ended and encourages an open-ended response. The person you are negotiating with will often blurt out damaging information, including how you were recommended, their current situation, why they are desperate for a deal, etc.

"How did you hear about us?" has the big advantage of being risk free. It is completely polite. It's innocent sounding and almost conversational. There is really no downside to asking this question as a matter of course. "How did you hear about us?" can and should be asked routinely by sellers of goods and services.

We have found that new potential clients almost always answer "How did you hear about us?" The reason for this is simple. The question is so innocent sounding and on its face so reasonable that the person you are negotiating with has no reason not to answer it. A sophisticated negotiator might be cagey when answering, but you are still very likely to get some sort of an answer.

Another important advantage of "How did you hear about us?" is that it allows sellers to track how various marketing campaigns are working. Let's say your business placed an ad in a certain newspaper and you routinely ask people calling to inquire about your services, "How did you hear about us?" If several people respond that they saw your ad in that newspaper, you know the ad worked and you might consider repeating it at a later time. If nobody mentions the ad you might consider discontinuing it.

The benefit of "How did you hear about us?" can be greatly enhanced if you ask follow-up questions. Once the person you are negotiating with starts answering one question it is more likely that they will answer follow-up questions. The conversation is flowing in this direction and the person you are negotiating with has already shown that they are willing to answer questions.

Asking the right follow-up questions depends on carefully listening to the responses you receive. The goal of all of this is to get the person you are negotiating with talking in the hopes that they will reveal information about why they called you, their situation, timetables, problems, budgets, or anything else that can be used to your advantage. Let's look at some examples.

Recently, we got a call from a person working at a federal governmental agency. He was interested in hiring us to train some of their employees. Here's how the negotiation went:

LEAD: Hi, I am interested in your company doing some training for us.
AUTHOR: That's great. How did you hear about us?
LEAD: One of our people here has been to your seminars and told us that your training is superb, that you are the best.

AUTHOR: What's your time frame for the training?
LEAD: Well, here's the thing. We have a lot of money we need to spend by October 1. So we'd like to move this along on the fast track.
AUTHOR: Well, we can certainly help you with your problem.

From the above example, you can see the potential phenomenal benefits of asking "How did you hear about us?" and innocuous follow-up questions. In response to "How did you hear about us?" we were able to learn the extremely valuable information that they already thought that we were the best. That is, they were already sold on us. The biggest and most valuable information score came on our follow-up question, "What's your time frame for the training?" The response we received about their having a ton of money they needed to spend fast was exactly the type of priceless information we were fishing for. Once we heard this answer, we were able to negotiate quickly and agree upon the highest fee we had ever collected for training.

Here's an additional example. Once again we were being contacted by an organization that was interested in hiring us to do some consulting/training.

LEAD: Hello, my group was interested in hiring you to do some consulting and training for us.
AUTHOR: Hi, nice to meet you. How did you hear about us?
LEAD: My boss is the president of the company. He's been to one of your seminars and loved it. He told me to hire you.
AUTHOR: That's very kind of him. Who's your boss?
LEAD: John Smith.

This also turned out to be a very easy negotiation. By asking the simple question "How did you hear about us?" we were able to learn that the potential client was already sold on us. More important, were able to discover that the person we were negotiating with basically had zero alternatives. He was actually instructed by his boss to use us. Needless to say, after learning this information, we were able to easily negotiate a favorable rate.

Lesson

Sellers should ask leads "How did you hear about us?" as a matter of course. This is a no-risk question that may result in valuable information being provided to you. The information often gained about the person you are negotiating with—motives, deadlines, budgets, intentions, etc.—can greatly enhance your negotiation position. This question can also help set up follow-up questions that can obtain additional useful information. "How did you hear about us?" has the additional important benefit of tracking the value of various marketing campaigns that you may have conducted.

How to Respond If You Are Asked "How did you hear about us?"

An excellent way to respond to this question if it is used against you is to provide an answer that suggests you are aggressively shopping around for the best deal. Such an answer will boost your bargaining power since the seller will likely draw the conclusion that he will have to offer the best deal in order to win your business. Please consider the following example, which is typical of the response we would give if we were asked "How did you hear about us?" by someone we were considering buying something from.

> **PRINTER:** How did you hear about us?
> **AUTHOR:** I had my assistant come up with a list of thirty to forty printers who do this type of work so that we could aggressively compare cost and get the lowest possible price.

Question #2

SO, HOW'S EVERYTHING GOING?

Your negotiating success is directly related to the amount and quality of the information that you are privy to. The more information you have the better your results will be. "So, how's everything going?" is a low-key, innocent-sounding question designed to help you learn valuable information from the person you are negotiating with. This question, and other small talk, is a good way to start many negotiations. In fact, it's the typical way we start many of our negotiations.

There are several variations of this question. These could include "So, how's business?" "What have you guys been up to?" "Have you been busy?" and the like. The idea is to ask a question that is friendly, conversational, and socially appropriate, and listen carefully to the response you get. You will be amazed at the valuable information the person may blurt out.

If used correctly, there is no downside to this question. The key to the risk-free use of this technique is to very gingerly question the person you are negotiating with and ask appropriate questions. Gentle questioning combined with careful listening can yield big dividends.

———

Here are two examples. In this first example, the question was actually used against us. Many years ago, one of the authors and his wife were negotiating to buy a new car with a dealer. Here's how the beginning of the discussions went after the test drive, as we sat down in his office to go over numbers:

SALESMAN: So, how are you folks doing?

AUTHOR AND SPOUSE: Fine. And you?

SALESMAN: Excellent. Where are you from?

AUTHOR AND SPOUSE: We're in the area.

SALESMAN: And what do you guys do for work?

AUTHOR AND SPOUSE: I work for a small business and my wife works at a bank.

SALESMAN: Did you guys go to school around here?

AUTHOR AND SPOUSE: Yes.

SALESMAN: Whereabouts?

AUTHOR AND SPOUSE: Boston. Look, we have two more dealers to visit tonight, so can we get down to how good of a bid you are going to have?

Since we are sophisticated negotiators we knew that we should be careful about providing information that was going to be against our interest. As such, we didn't leap out and volunteer that we lived in an upscale town and were both lawyers who went to prestigious schools. Two high-powered lawyers usually don't get much sympathy when claiming that they can't afford something or that they need to be cost-conscious. What we did reveal is that we were going to be shopping around to other dealers. This was intentionally done to improve our negotiating position.

Here's another example. In 2009, one of the authors and his spouse were vacationing on Martha's Vineyard. It was near the end of the summer. The great recession was still in force. While traveling, the author's wife had just lost a prized bracelet that she had worn every day for the last twenty years. We walked into a jewelry store that she liked with the aim of seeing if we could find a replacement.

> **JEWELER:** How are you folks doing?
> **AUTHOR'S WIFE:** We are having a pleasant trip, thank you. How are things going for you?
> **JEWELER:** We're hanging in there.
> **AUTHOR'S WIFE:** How's business been?
> **JEWELER:** It's been a tough summer.
> **AUTHOR'S WIFE:** Yeah, I hear you. When does your peak season end?
> **JEWELER:** Next weekend, unfortunately. If you are interested in anything, please let me know.

After asking these questions the author's wife had a very good idea that she could negotiate a tough bargain if she found anything she was interested in. Business was tough and the season was almost over. She, in fact, found a bracelet that she very much liked. There was a $500 price tag on it and she was prepared.

> **AUTHOR'S WIFE:** How much flexibility do you have in the price on this?*
> **JEWELER:** We can come down 50 percent.
> **AUTHOR'S WIFE:** What does that come to with tax?
> **JEWELER:** $265.63.
> **AUTHOR'S WIFE:** I don't know. We're heading to Edgartown tomorrow, there's a lot of nice jewelry stores there. If you make it $200 *including the tax,* you've got yourself a deal.
> **JEWELER:** Let me call my boss.

* See Question #26.

Ten minutes later the author's wife walked out with the new bracelet for a price more than 60 percent off the asking price. She's worn it daily since. Her small-talk questioning, "So how's business?" yielded invaluable information as to how desperate the store was to raise cash before the long cold winter. As such, she was able to push aggressively on price. This was set up by questions designed to promote anxiety such as asking when the jeweler's high season ended. Her not volunteering that she was looking to buy in response to the jeweler's small-talk question, "How are you folks doing?" also helped improve her bargaining position.

Lesson

Every communication made with someone you may end up negotiating with should be considered part of the negotiation. As such, the gathering and control of information should be a prime concern of yours. Small-talk questions such as "So, how's everything going?" and "How's business been?" are risk free and can provide you with valuable information.

How to Respond If You Are Asked "So, how's everything going?"

The person you are negotiating with will likely also use these questions against you. When he does, you should be careful not to reveal information that will weaken your negotiating position. Instead, you should use the opportunity of being asked such an open-ended question to strengthen your negotiating position by providing answers that will do so. For example:

> **BUYER:** So, how's it going?
> **SELLER:** Excellent, thank you. My only complaint is that I haven't been able to take as much time off as I would like; it's been very busy and we're just trying to keep up with the demand. How's it going with you?

Question #3

WHAT IS YOUR TIME FRAME FOR WRAPPING UP THIS NEGOTIATION?

This is a superb question to ask in almost any negotiation since it is very innocent sounding and can often provide you with valuable information. Information, of course, translates into leverage, which translates into better negotiation results. The other benefit of this question is that the person you are negotiating with is reminded of the pressures that he or she is under to finalize a deal.

A good time to ask "What is your time frame for wrapping up this negotiation?" is toward the beginning of the negotiation. The answer that you receive can help determine how you proceed with the rest of the negotiation. The types of answers you will typically receive are:

Nonresponsive or evasive: "I haven't thought about that. What's yours?" This type of response probably reveals that you are dealing with a sophisticated negotiator who does not readily leak information unless such leaks are intentional.

Snappy or defensive: "That's none of your business." This is a helpful response in that it helps you to identify parties that you wouldn't want to get involved with.

Honest and direct: "I really would like to wrap this up before the end of the quarter. That is, by close of business tomorrow." This is a very helpful response as it shows that the person you are negotiating with is eager to conclude an agreement and is operating under time pressure.

The answer you are hoping for, of course, is the honest and direct one. You'd be surprised how often the person you are negotiating with will blurt out revealing and valuable information in response to your question "What is your time frame for wrapping up this negotiation?"

We have been using this question for years to great effect. One memorable occasion involved our negotiating with a major corporation about training part of their staff in legal matters. Once again, toward the beginning of the negotiation and before we set our price, we asked the question, "What is your time frame for wrapping up this negotiation?" The answer that came directly resulted in our being able to command a premium fee. "We're under a court order to complete this training in the next ninety days so we'd like to nail this down immediately, if possible." There certainly could have been other questions we could have asked that would have resulted in this information being leaked, but the beauty of this question is that it is very innocent sounding.

A second example. One of the authors and his spouse were negotiating to buy a house. We had agreed on a price but were still negotiating the terms of the purchase and sale agreement. These terms, of course, can be quite important. We had been going back and forth for a while and there were some potentially deal-breaking issues that we had not reached agreement on, such as precise inspection contingency language, how clear the seller's title needed to be, language dealing with the septic system inspection, the closing date, etc. We asked the seller's agent what his time frame was for wrapping this up. His answer came back: "The sellers are down in Florida closing on their new house today, so I hope to be able to get an answer from them sometime tomorrow." Again, very helpful information was revealed. The fact that the sellers were now locked into their new house purchase gave us much more leverage in the purchase and sale agreement. We were able to resolve the negotiation favorably. The bottom line is that you never know what kind of helpful information will be leaked by the person you are negotiating with as a result of an innocent-sounding question such as "What is your time frame for wrapping up this negotiation?"

Lesson

"What is your time frame for wrapping up this negotiation?" is a great question to ask in that there is very little risk in asking the question, it is innocent sounding, and it may often result in your being provided with valuable information that directly leads to a more favorable negotiating result.

How to Respond If You Are Asked "What is your time frame for wrapping up this negotiation?"

First and foremost, you don't want to reveal any information that suggests you are pressed for time. Ideally, you will respond to this question in a way that turns the pressure around and suggests that the person you are negotiating with had better come up with a great deal quickly or they will be out of luck. Please consider the following example where we used this question as an opportunity to reinforce to the seller that we were shopping around and, as such, would need a great offer in order to buy from this seller.

> **SELLER:** What is your time frame for wrapping this up?
> **AUTHORS:** Well, we have numerous bids in hand, so if you want to be in the running, we'd need something by close of business tomorrow.

Alternatively, you could make a statement suggestive of your being in no rush because you haven't even made a decision that you need to buy yet. Such a response will also help your bargaining position since the seller will have to offer you enough to convince you take action. For example:

> **SELLER:** What is your time frame for wrapping this up?
> **AUTHORS:** We're in no rush. Unless we get a really good bid, we probably will just forgo for now.

PART II

The Right Person

INTRODUCTION: It is very important when negotiating to understand the importance of dealing with the right person. You will usually get far better results by dealing with as senior a person as possible. The questions in this section are designed to help you get you to the right person, who can give you the best possible deal.

Question #4

WHOM DO I SPEAK WITH ABOUT CANCELING OUR SERVICE?

A good negotiator should always keep in mind the value of a long-term relationship. If you are a long-term customer or client, you often have tremendous negotiating leverage with your vendor. The reason for this is clear. If you are spending, say, $100 a month on a vendor, this account is worth $12,000 to the vendor over the next ten years. Not only that, since the vendor need not spend any additional marketing dollars to generate the revenue from you, the profit the vendor makes from you can be relatively large. What all this means is that the vendor has every economic incentive to do what is necessary to keep you as a client or as a customer.

The impact of being able to negotiate a better deal from a long-term vendor must be appreciated. In the above example of a $100-a-month vendor (say, a cable company), saving 20 percent off your bill translates into $240 a year or $2,400 over ten years.

"Whom do I speak with about canceling our service?" is a superb question to use to get a better deal from a longtime vendor. Your vendors understand how much you are worth to them and do not want to lose you. We have found that this question works well even with huge companies such as cable and phone companies, whom you would not think you could negotiate with. In fact, many large companies will agree to concessions only after this question has been asked. Such companies may even have special "customer retention" employees who are specially empowered to give deals.

To be most effective, "Whom do I speak with about canceling our service?" should be asked in a very polite, almost apologetic fashion. The person you direct this question to will be more likely to respond favorably if he/she finds you polite and likeable. It is also a good idea to set up your asking of this question by reiterating how much you have enjoyed the vendor's product or services. This will make you appear to be a satisfied customer who will continue with the vendor for the long term if the vendor can get you a better deal.

Another way to increase the likelihood of success is to preface your question with either an explanation of why you are forced to save money (stock market crashed, the boss has implemented across-the-board budget cuts, some crisis). This makes your implied threat of firing the vendor much more believable.

A final technique that can be used to increase the odds of this question working is to do your homework about competing services. When you negotiate, your explanation or leverage is usually going to be either "We'll just do without it" or "We found a better deal from your competitor." Mentioning a better deal from a competitor will greatly increase your leverage when using this question.

We have successfully used this question or a variation thereof (e.g., "I'm thinking about canceling our service; what would I need to do this?") in a variety of circumstances. Here are some examples.

When the 2008 financial crisis hit after the collapse of Lehman Brothers, we immediately saw the writing on the wall and went into an aggressive cost-saving mode. We appointed a point person to look at all our long-term deals and try to reduce costs. Through the use of this question we were able to produce superb results, which meant that we did not have to lay off any employees.

One of our greatest continuing costs is credit-card fees. When a customer uses a credit card to buy something from us, the credit-card company charges a percentage of the sales price to us as a processing fee. So, if the customer spent $100, we'd get only, say, $97, and the credit-card company skims $3 or 3 percent off the top. In a company with multimillion-dollar sales these credit-card fees can really add up. For example, if we had $2,000,000 in credit-card fees in a year, saving 1 percent in fees on each transaction would add another $20,000 to our bottom line.

We called up the credit-card processing company to get a better deal. We went back and forth. Eventually they offered to lower our fee by a paltry one-tenth of a percent, figuring we'd be happy with that. We weren't. So we asked, "Whom do I speak with about canceling our service?" The response came back that somebody would call us back within twenty-four hours. We got a call the next day with an immediate offer to lower our fees by one full percentage point per transaction. It was quite obvious that the person who called us had the job of making sure the credit-card processing company didn't lose any customers. This is ten times the concession we had previously received in all our negotiating and has saved us tens of thousands of dollars per year since. Over ten years, this one question will have made us hundreds of thousands of dollars in additional profits.

We used this question very successfully with our other vendors as well. In fact, there was not one long-term vendor with whom we used this question that we were not able to obtain a better deal. Here's how it went with the phone company. (Keep in mind that because of the disruption involved we really did not want to switch to a different service provider.)

AUTHOR (CUSTOMER): Good morning. How are you?

PHONE COMPANY REP 1: Fine, sir, and you?

AUTHOR (CUSTOMER): Hanging in there, times have been tough.

PHONE COMPANY REP 1: I am sorry to hear that. How can I help you?

AUTHOR (CUSTOMER): I have been put in charge of saving money for the company and am calling to see if I can get a better deal.

PHONE COMPANY REP 1: Oh, certainly, I can help you with that. Let me see. If you sign up for a new two-year commitment we can drop your rate $5 month.

AUTHOR (CUSTOMER): Okay. That's not what we had in mind. I see your competitor here is offering these services for 30 percent less. Whom do I talk to about canceling our service so I can switch to them?

PHONE COMPANY REP 1: I am glad you mentioned canceling and our competitor. Now I can transfer you to our retention department. I think they'll be able to take good care of you.

AUTHOR (CUSTOMER): Okay, thank you very much.

PHONE COMPANY REP 2: Good morning, Mr. Mangraviti. I am sorry to hear you were thinking of canceling your account.

AUTHOR (CUSTOMER): Yes. Unfortunately, these times have been tough. We like your service, but I see your competitors are offering a better deal, so I was wondering what I needed to do to cancel. Do you need something in writing or whatnot?

PHONE COMPANY REP 2: I'll tell you what. What if we reduced your rate by 35 percent for the next twelve months? Would that keep you on board?

AUTHOR (CUSTOMER): Thank you. If you could do that, we'd have no reason to switch.

PHONE COMPANY REP 2: Done. If you have any other problems or concerns, please don't hesitate to give me a call.

The phone company is obviously a very large organization. Note that they had a special department to handle persons threatening cancellations and that that department was authorized to make significant concessions.

As a final example, here's how it went with our bottled-water company. Notice two things. One, we were prepared to explain (believably) that we would simply go without their service, which was more of a luxury. Second, the company was willing to go to somewhat extreme lengths to keep us as a customer.

AUTHOR (CUSTOMER): Whom do I speak to about canceling our service?

BOTTLED-WATER COMPANY: That would be me. I see you have been a good customer for twelve years. What seems to be the problem? Is it service?

AUTHOR (CUSTOMER): No, not really. The water comes very regularly. Sometimes they leave a bit more than we need—but the real reason I called is that our company has decided in these difficult economic times to cut back on items and services we don't need in order to keep going, and bottled water is on the list.

BOTTLED-WATER COMPANY: I am sorry to hear that. I might be able to give you a better deal if that would help?

AUTHOR (CUSTOMER): What do you have in mind?

BOTTLED-WATER COMPANY: I could give you a high-use volume discount, although you technically don't qualify for it.

AUTHOR (CUSTOMER): What are we talking about in dollars and cents?

BOTTLED-WATER COMPANY: It would take your bill down from $500 a month to $300 a month with no decrease in volume or service.

AUTHOR (CUSTOMER): How come you never offered this to us before? We have been getting water for the past twelve years.

BOTTLED-WATER COMPANY: In fairness, you did not qualify for the volume discount and you never really asked for it.

AUTHOR (CUSTOMER): I like the reduction to $300 a month, but what about something to sweeten the deal?

BOTTLED-WATER COMPANY: Would two months' free product make you a happy customer again?

AUTHOR (CUSTOMER): I am starting to smile—for four months I would be happy.

BOTTLED-WATER COMPANY: I will get you the four months' free product. I hope you continue to enjoy our product.

Lesson

Never underestimate the negotiating leverage you have with long-term vendors. Your business is tremendously valuable to them. "Whom do I speak to about canceling our service?" can be the simple key to unlocking more favorable deals that can add up to huge savings over time.

How to Respond If You Are Asked "Whom do I speak to about canceling our service?"

As a businessperson, you usually don't want to lose a customer. We hate to get calls from customers asking to sever their relationship with us. To avoid getting calls like this we focus as hard we can on providing superior value to our clients, such that the last thing our clients want to do is cancel their service with us.

When we do receive calls regarding canceling, our response is to ask why they are canceling. If there is a problem we can fix or a misunderstanding (there often is), we will try to fix it.

A method that has worked for us is to view this as an opportunity to identify a problem and fix it. So our answer is, "What seems to be the problem and how can we make it right?" When the problem is legitimate (our fault) and the proposed solution is reasonable, we make it right and build an even stronger relationship with the customer.

If the customer truly isn't satisfied with our service, we don't argue. We cancel and give them whatever refund they are due. What we won't do is start negotiating or lowering our price, which is a slippery slope that can get very much out of hand if word gets out.

Question #5

DO YOU HAVE FULL AUTHORITY
TO NEGOTIATE AND FINALIZE A DEAL?

Your goal in negotiating is to gain concessions and a good deal. Negotiating with someone who is not authorized to grant you concessions is a losing proposition since you have nothing to gain and much to lose. "Do you have full authority to negotiate and finalize a deal?" is designed to determine quickly and easily how much authority the person you are negotiating with has. The subtexts of this question are simple: We can only finalize a deal if you are fully authorized to negotiate. We need to negotiate, what is on the table is not acceptable to me. I am ready to make a deal if I can get additional concessions.

In order to be a superior negotiator, you must be familiar with the concept of trickle-down loss. Here's what we mean by trickle-down loss. Let's say you are negotiating to buy something. You deal with a salesperson who reports to a sales director. The sales director reports to the vice president of sales. The vice president of sales knows that the company's bottom line on selling the item in question is $100. He tells this to the sales director. The sales director wants to look good in front of his boss, so the sales director tells the salesperson not to sell for lower than $110. The salesperson wants to look good in front of his boss, the sales director, so he decides that he can't sell the item for less than $120. This is the essence of trickle-down loss. Each person involved in the chain of authority wants to impress his boss. Each person involved in the chain of authority costs you money.

Dealing with a person who does not have full authority to make concessions may also slow things down considerably. Each concession will have to be run up the flagpole and justified and approved by superiors. The more often the person you are negotiating with has to call his superiors to get permission to make concessions, the more protracted the negotiation and the less likely you are to get meaningful concessions.

Keep in mind as well that dealing with someone without full authority to make concessions is a one-way street heading in the wrong direction. You will be asked to make concessions, but you cannot receive anything in return. Negotiating against yourself like this is a losing proposition that can be avoided by making sure you deal only with someone who has full authority to negotiate.

It is crucially important to determine as early as possible how much authority the person you are negotiating with actually has. As such, "Do you have full authority to negotiate and finalize a deal?" is best asked at the beginning of a negotiation. If you receive a positive reply, you can begin the give-and-take of negotiating. If, on the other hand, you receive a negative reply you should politely ask to deal with the person who does have full authority to negotiate.

An alternative way to find the person with full authority to negotiate is to ask, "Who is the decision maker in your organization?" If the answer comes back that it is the person you are negotiating with, you can proceed with the negotiation. If the answer comes back that the decision maker is someone else, you should politely but firmly ask to speak with the decision maker.

We use this technique routinely in our own business. We have found that we get far better deals (and get them much more quickly) when we deal with the person with the ultimate authority in an organization. To take advantage of this concept we strongly prefer to deal with small to midsize organizations where we can reach agreements on a principal-to-principal basis. For example, we purposefully seek out independently owned hotels in which to run our seminars and conferences. Such ownership allows us to negotiate on a principal-to-principal basis and obtain far better deals. For example, a few years ago, we started to explore entering a relationship with a family-owned hotel in Florida. Here's about how the negotiation went.

AUTHORS: We came here today from Cape Cod, Massachusetts, to Florida, to talk about your proposed hotel contract. As you know, there are three areas of concern that we had.

MANAGER: That is our standard contract. Nothing I can do about it.

AUTHORS: Do you have authority to negotiate and finalize a deal with us?

MANAGER: I already told you, no—it is standard.

AUTHORS: One of the reasons we selected this hotel and traveled 1,200 miles is because it is a family-run business like our own; could you bring the owner down here to meet with us?

MANAGER: I don't normally like to bother him; he has had some health issues. Let me see if I can reach him on his cell phone.

OWNER: What seems to be the problem here?

AUTHORS: We are a family-run company like yours; we have been in business twenty-nine years and I understand your family has run this hotel for forty-five years, congratulations. We are looking at your hotel for our annual Florida conferences, but we have reached a bit of a sticking point.

OWNER: What sticking point?

AUTHORS: We have issue with these three clauses in your standard contract. . . .

OWNER (TO MANAGER): How is their credit rating and history?
MANAGER: A-one—as near to perfect as you could find. But the clauses they are talking about are standard in all—
OWNER (TO MANAGER): Waive the three clauses and let's get these fine gentlemen from Cape Cod some grouper.

The results in this example are fairly typical. You generally can make much greater headway dealing with the decision maker in an organization. A low-level person must follow rules and procedures and is very afraid of looking bad in front of his boss by giving away too much. In order to have the best chance of the most meaningful concessions, you should strive to negotiate with a person with full authority, if possible, the owner himself. Asking "Do you have the full authority to negotiate and finalize a deal?" at the beginning of a negotiation is a simple way to get to a person with full authority.

Lesson

Determining the authority of the person you are negotiating with is crucial for a successful outcome. Negotiating with a person who has lesser authority will result in worse terms. It will also slow down the negotiations. "Do you have the full authority to negotiate and finalize a deal?" is a simple and effective way to determine if you are negotiating with a person who has full authority. When you don't have such a person, politely, but firmly, ask to talk to someone with full authority.

How to Respond If You Are Asked "Do you have the full authority to negotiate and finalize a deal?"

This is a question that should not be answered with a "yes" or "no." A "yes" gives you no wiggle room. A "no" will prompt a request to talk to someone with full authority. To answer this question we suggest that you dispute the very premise of the question that there is *anybody* who has full authority. For example, "Nobody has full authority here, all my partners need to sign off on everything," or "I would, of course, need to consult with my spouse before we could finalize anything."

Question #6

MAY I PLEASE SPEAK TO YOUR SUPERVISOR?

It is very common to run into a stone wall when you are negotiating for something that you want or need. This stone wall often comes in the form of a low-level front-line employee who states that they can't give you what you want or need. If you ever run into such a stone wall a good way to go around it is to simply ask, "May I please speak to your supervisor?"

Asking "May I please speak to your supervisor?" when you have reached a deadlock can be very effective at leading to the result you need or want. The key is to get yourself connected with a person who has authority to grant your request. Trying to negotiate with someone who does not have the power to grant what you want is futile. "May I please speak to your supervisor?" should be deployed as soon as you determine that the low-level person you are talking with cannot or will not help you.

One benefit of asking "May I please speak to your supervisor?" is that it is very low risk. The person you are asking this to will almost always say "yes." The reasons for this are that they have usually been trained to do so and that they are frankly glad to pass along someone that they cannot make happy. Since the worst the person you first talk to can say is "no," there is really little to no risk in asking this question.

Once you have been passed on to a supervisor you will need to plead your case for what you are looking for. The more persuasive your arguments, the more likely it is that you will get what you are looking for. We have used this question to great effect many times over the years. Here are just a few examples:

A few years ago, one of the authors and his wife bought a new house. We're very organized people, so after the purchase and sale agreement had been signed and a closing date had been set, we started making arrangements to get our ducks in a row. One of the first calls we made was to the phone company. We talked to a very nice representative, picked out an easy-to-remember phone number, and scheduled service to begin the day after closing. In the meantime, we sent out notices to all our friends and family with our new contact information and telephone number. More important, we contacted all of our credit-card companies, financial companies, rewards programs, etc., with our new information. This was a very time-consuming process that probably took us six or seven hours.

We closed on the house as scheduled and the next day the phone company showed up right on time. The tech was very nice and he spent three or four hours getting the lines all set up. Before he left I tried out the line by calling my cell phone. I was puzzled to see a different number than we had reserved come up on caller ID. I told the tech he had given us the wrong number and why this was a big deal to us. The tech told me there was nothing he could do, this was the number he was told to put in. Needless to say I wasn't happy. I had quite a lot going on at that point and didn't have another six or seven hours to notify everybody all over again.

I asked to speak to the tech's supervisor and he gave me a number to call. The woman who responded was not helpful. She said there was nothing that she could do, and they don't guarantee the numbers until day of installation. I explained that nobody had ever told me that and that I had spent all this time notifying people and would have to do it all over again. Having had enough, I asked, "May I please speak to your supervisor?" She was happy to be rid of me and put me through to her boss. I pled my case and finally got back an acceptable answer of "Let me see what I can do." In two days we had the number that we had reserved back. If we hadn't asked for a supervisor we never would have gotten what we needed.

One of the authors had a similar experience with an airline many years back. I knew I had to be someplace on a certain date. A full six months in advance, I called to redeem some frequent-flier points to get a seat on a certain flight. I was told that there were no more reward seats available on that flight. This was obviously untrue since the flight had just started taking reservations. How could it possibly be sold out for rewards unless their whole program was a scam? I got nowhere pleading my case with the first person who answered, so I asked, "May I please speak to your supervisor?" The supervisor came on and within five minutes I was granted the tickets I was looking for.

One final story. Very recently, one of the authors and his spouse were out to breakfast at a local restaurant. We were redeeming a gift certificate that I had received for my birthday. The kitchen was ridiculously slow (more than an hour for scrambled eggs), but the food was good and the waitress was very nice. The bill came to $21 and we handed over the gift certificate for $40. We received back the gift certificate with a new amount of $19 on it. So we asked, "Can't we include the tip on this?" This is a very reasonable request. We've never seen a restaurant not do this. The waitress said that this was only her second day and that she was told that we couldn't do that. We immediately asked her, "May I please speak to the owner?" Now that we were talking to the right person, we made our points and the owner agreed to pull the tip from the gift certificate.

Lesson

Negotiating with someone who will not or cannot give you what you need is a futile proposition. If you want or need something and run into a stone wall, you will often have much better luck obtaining what you want if you talk to someone higher up the chain of command. "May I please speak to your supervisor?" is a simple, easy, and risk-free way to get to the person who can or will say "yes" to your requests. This question can be particularly effective when dealing with large, seemingly inflexible organizations such as telecommunication companies, airlines, and financial institutions.

How to Respond If You Are Asked "May I please speak to your supervisor?"

If you have a supervisor, the best way to respond to this question is just to say "Yes, absolutely." Refusing will only make the person you are negotiating with even more upset. Since you can't give the person what he wants, it's a waste of time to keep dealing with him.

In our business, if anyone asks, we will immediately put him through to the CEO/owner of our company. Such a response shows that we have nothing to hide and that we take a dissatisfied customer very seriously.

PART III

Opening Moves

INTRODUCTION: You will often obtain superior results in negotiations if you are able to get off to a strong start. A strong start can set the tone for the negotiation, help you develop power, and dictate the parameters of what will and will not be open to discussion. The questions in this part are designed to be used at the beginning of a negotiation.

Question #7

CAN YOU SHOOT ME AN E-MAIL BEFORE THE MEETING WITH YOUR ISSUES, GOALS, AND CONCERNS SO I CAN PREPARE?

Successful negotiation results are highly dependent on the amount of leverage you have or can gain during the negotiation. One way to gain leverage is through information. An effective way to gather information is simply to ask for it. The question "Can you shoot me an e-mail before the meeting with your issues, goals, and concerns so I can prepare?" is designed to effectively and innocuously gather information that you can use to your advantage during a negotiation.

The reason that this question works so well is that it often results in the person you are negotiating with revealing a treasure trove of crucial information, data, and omissions, including:

- Their specific goals and concerns, often with clues as to which are most important to them

- Key facts that you can use to your advantage

- Issues that the person you are negotiating with feels are important to address

- Issues that you thought might be important, which are not even listed

This question works best when you have some inherent control over the situation and the person you are going to be meeting with is looking to do business with you. We as a rule use "Can you shoot me an e-mail before the meeting with your issues, goals, and concerns so I can prepare?" in the context of our business when someone approaches us out of the blue and wants to talk business, usually about a joint venture or some sort of collaborative relationship. Since we have been in business for thirty years, we get many such requests for meetings each year. Usually these requests are from less mature businesses, start-ups, or individuals who want or need our help to take their business up to the next level. They usually hope to do this by somehow accessing our customer base, using our reputation, or asking us to hire them or buy their product.

Meetings with other people to discuss possibly doing business together can often quickly turn into negotiating sessions or can be a precursor to serious and important negotiations. Either way, finding out as much information as possible from the other party is very important. An added benefit of asking "Can you shoot me an e-mail before the meeting with your issues, goals, and concerns so I can prepare?" is that if the reply is that the person won't send the e-mail or the person sends an e-mail describing a proposal of zero interest, you can save your valuable time and cancel the meeting before it even takes place.

The subtext of "Can you shoot me an e-mail before the meeting with your issues, goals, and concerns so I can prepare?" is simple: Help me help you. Its beauty lies in its inherent reasonableness, in other words, "How can I possible come prepared to the negotiation if I don't know what your goals and issues are?" Requesting an e-mail from the party who has approached you to possibly do some business has worked well for us for many reasons, including:

- It is logical and seems to be in the recipient's best interest. The phrase "so I can prepare" implies that you are taking things seriously and are considering making a deal. The person you are dealing with will want you to be prepared and focused on them for the meeting. They should also want to impress you.

- You are asking for an e-mail, not a formal contract or proposal. People tend to be informal in e-mails. E-mails are usually not drafted with the caution someone would employ when drafting a formal contract or proposal. In addition, many people rush responses to e-mails, such as responding from a smart phone while on the move or while they are distracted by other things. As such, the person you will be meeting with is more likely to leak information of use to you than if you had asked for a formal proposal.

- The person you are dealing with will understand that the failure to cooperate and respond to such an innocuous request may be offensive and result in their not being able to keep their meeting with you.

- The person you are dealing with may believe that their framing the issues and goals of the meeting would probably be to their own advantage since they can steer the conversation to their areas of interest and have a better shot at getting what they want.

We also use the question "Can you shoot me an e-mail before the meeting with your issues, goals, and concerns so I can prepare?" when we are involved in ongoing or formal negotiations with someone whom we actually know we would want to do business with. Here the issue is simply coming to terms. In this scenario, the question is designed to gather information. The goal, of course, is to use the information gathered by the question to our advantage.

Let's look at some examples of where we have used this question very effectively. The first involves the most common scenario. We are approached by a start-up venture, an individual, or a less mature business to set up a meeting to talk since "we should be working together." We typically entertain such entrees but always ask, "Can you shoot me an e-mail before the meeting with your issues, goals, and concerns so I can prepare?" We often get a response like this:

> Hi, Steve and Jim,
> My pleasure. We have some great products. You have a fantastic reputation, loyal customer base, and a Web site and store with large amounts of traffic. I'd like to discuss how you could make a lot of money if you could give me access to your e-mail list and we could get our products up on your Web site. Look very much forward to meeting with you.
> Regards,
> Charlie

For privacy and other reasons we would never grant anyone access to our customer lists. For other business reasons, including diluting the sales of our own higher-margin products, we do not sell other company's products on our Web store. As such, we really wouldn't have anything to talk about with Charlie and would reply something like this:

Dear Charlie:
Thank you for your note. Because of privacy concerns and
corporate policy what you propose is not possible and we
will need to cancel our tentative meeting. We wish you the
best with your project.
    All the best,
    Steve and Jim

Asking the simple question "Can you shoot me an e-mail before the meeting with your issues, goals, and concerns so I can prepare?" quickly and respectfully smoked out what the person was after and saved us the time we would have wasted meeting with him.

Here's a second example. In this case, asking the question helped get us a superior deal. A few years back we received an unsolicited résumé and cover letter from a high-powered lawyer who had just retired to Cape Cod, where we are based. The lawyer (we'll call him Robert), summed up his qualifications and was requesting a meeting to discuss our working together.

We believe that having the right talent can be one of the key drivers of success and failure in a business. From the résumé and cover letter we received, Robert appeared to be talent that could help make us money. Based on Cape Cod where we are, we usually don't have the same access to talent that you would have in a big city like Boston.

The problem with talent, of course, is that you have to pay for it. We suspected, but did not know, that Robert would be too expensive for us. One of the biggest mistakes in negotiating is assuming that you know what the other person wants. We agreed to a lunch meeting with Robert, but first we asked him, "Can you shoot us an e-mail before the meeting with your issues, goals, and concerns so we can prepare?"

The answer came back something like this:

> *Dear Steve and Jim:*
> *Thank you so much for agreeing to meet with me. I have*
> *studied your Web page and am fascinated and impressed*
> *with what you have done.*
> *After six months of retirement I am going a little*
> *stir-crazy and am looking for a way to get out of the house*
> *a couple of days a week, to challenge the brain, and to do*
> *something a little bit different. I thought that a person with*
> *my background and experience might be of use to you and*
> *wanted to discuss how we might be able to work together.*
> *I look forward to seeing you for lunch on Friday.*
> *Robert*

We very much liked the response Robert gave since it tended to indicate that money was not a primary concern and he was not looking for full-time work. As such, he might be affordable to us. We went forward with the lunch meeting and indeed were able to hire Robert on a contract basis for short money. Robert successfully and very cost-effectively tackled a project that he was uniquely qualified to complete. Asking for the e-mail resulted in the information that he wasn't overly interested in money and allowed us to reach a mutually beneficial arrangement.

Here's a final example where this question was used as part of ongoing negotiations. A few years back we were hired as professional negotiating consultants by a medical society to help negotiate a new contract with a publisher for their journal. These were very complex and lengthy seven-figure negotiations, the technical details of which are not important for this discussion. Prior to one of our series of meetings with one of the publishers we asked, "Can you shoot me an e-mail before the meeting with your issues, goals, and concerns so I can prepare?" The response came back something like this and vastly increased our leverage:

We have several issues:

1. *Determine the expenses you incurred when you gave us your profit numbers. Specifically, which one of the following items did you include: paper, printing, binding, postage, editorial, administration and management, production, order fulfillment, selling and marketing, and general administrative (legal, accounting, management, and corporate overhead)?*

2. *What did you include as part of total revenue? Were all the following items included: all subscriptions, sponsored subscriptions, electronic searches and databases, reprints (commercial and author), back issues, color charges, pay-per-view, rights permissions, and collections of part articles converted to books/ monographs?*

3. *Which of the following items do you feel we can reasonably increase revenue in: article reprints, belly bands, classified advertising, journal supplements, patient education tablets, premium positions, and special sales?*
   As we have been at this for three months, our goal, quite frankly, is to wrap this up within two weeks.

Items 1 and 2 we came prepared to answer factually. Item 3 we came prepared with responses that helped our client. The truly valuable information was clearly the last sentence, which telegraphed to us how highly invested the publisher was in the deal, suggested a level of desperation, and also suggested that the publisher might be up against an internal deadline. After receiving this e-mail we made the conscious and calculated decision to harden our demands. Our read of their situation turned out to be 100 percent correct and we were able to obtain an extremely lucrative deal for our clients.

Lesson

Knowledge in a negotiation is power. Asking "Can you shoot me an e-mail before the meeting with your issues, goals, and concerns so I can prepare?" can increase your power by helping to provide you with valuable information. It can also help you to get inside the head of the person you are negotiating with. The question is most commonly used when someone is approaching you with a business proposition. It can also be used in ongoing negotiations prior to a formal negotiating session. An additional benefit of this question is that it can be used to help you screen out persons it would not be worth your time to meet with in person.

How to Respond If You Are Asked "Can you shoot me an e-mail before the meeting with your issues, goals, and concerns so I can prepare?"

If you are approaching someone with the hopes of doing business, a negative response risks their canceling the meeting and should be avoided. As we have seen above, a specific response can be used against you. Accordingly, the best response you can come up with to this question is usually a vague one. For example, "I would like to explore all avenues of potential synergy where we could possibly produce a win-win relationship." Hopefully, such a murky response will be sufficient. If the other party pushes for specificity, you may need to provide specifics so that the other party does not cancel the meeting. For example, "We have three additional ways to sell your books at no out-of-pocket cost to your company—can we meet so that I may explain them to you?"

If, on the other hand, you are dealing with someone who you suspect wants to talk to you, a good way to respond to this question is to try to turn it around. For example, "This is an excellent idea. I would be happy to. If you could, please send me an e-mail with your issues, concerns, and goals, and I will respond to each one of them and add in anything else that I feel might be helpful." The idea here is to try to turn the question against the person who asked it. Note that the way this sample response is phrased makes it actually appear that you are trying to help the other person.

Question #8

I WILL SEND OUT A PROPOSED AGENDA, OKAY?

One of the first things the authors learned in business is that if you would like to have a disproportionately greater impact on the results of a meeting (which really is a negotiation), it is usually best to try to control the agenda. We also learned pretty early on that having and controlling an agenda can greatly help push things to a conclusion and avoid wasting valuable time.

Setting an agenda in the context of a negotiation can be quite helpful. Asking "I will send out a proposed agenda, okay?" is a simple and innocuous way to try to get the person you are negotiating with to agree to your setting the agenda. The question seems very reasonable since you appear to be taking on extra work. The reasons that having an agenda and setting and controlling the contents of the agenda are important and include:

- **The agenda controls what issues will be discussed, and more important, the order in which they will be discussed.**

- A well-drafted agenda can minimize conflict until rapport and buy-in of the parties is achieved. As such we recommend scheduling at the beginning of the session items that will put the other party at ease (such as, by stroking their ego) and that make you and your team appear in a very favorable light. It's also a good idea to begin the agenda with items that are "low-hanging fruit" and that are not really in dispute, such as common goals and assumptions. Achieving early success on items will help build rapport, momentum, and the expectation of success.

- Since you are setting the agenda you can highlight areas of strength where you have the most knowledge and where you are best prepared to carry the day.

- Having an agenda explicitly or implicitly creates one or a series of deadlines. Deadlines make things happen in a negotiation. Concessions generally increase when the parties are up against a time deadline and an agenda creates one or more deadlines.

- Including the recipient's issues (or most of them) demonstrates fairness and evenhandedness, which will be appreciated by the person(s) you are negotiating with.

- Leaving space in the agenda for issues that others may be interested in shows your flexibility and should increase the other party's desire to do business with you.

"I will send out a proposed agenda, okay?" is best used in situations where you would like to push the negotiation process to an ultimate conclusion. Incalculable time and money can be lost in endless negotiations and meetings. Setting an agenda is designed to bring things to a conclusion. That conclusion could, of course, be that you can't reach a favorable agreement. In many cases however, this is fine. You'll want to know this as soon as possible so that you can move on and stop wasting valuable time in pointless negotiation sessions.

Note that agendas need to be carefully drafted. You do not want to include in an agenda any information likely to decrease your negotiating leverage such as "Item #4: Urgency to close deal quickly." It is also important to avoid distractions, minutiae, and avoidable divisive issues. An agenda that contains too many items, ancillary issues, and divisive issues not likely to be resolved can result in delay or a deadlock.

"I will send out a proposed agenda, okay?" is most likely to work where the other party is inexperienced, lazy, busy, or distracted. It goes without saying that the absolute best time to ask the question is shortly before the meeting.

One final point before we go over some examples. Try to remember that not all negotiations are about buying or selling. When committees and teams work collaboratively to come up with a consensus course of action, this is in fact a negotiation. Spouses negotiate in this way all the time. So do lawmakers. "I will send out a proposed agenda, okay?" is a great question to ask in these types of negotiations that do not involve buying or selling. Also note that just because buying and selling is not directly involved does not mean that there will not be potentially huge financial consequences to a negotiation.

Let's look at some examples. Many years ago, we had an executive summit with all our firm's top management. The idea was to plan out what we would be doing in sales, marketing, and product development for the next one to two years. Obviously, these were decisions of extreme importance.

One of the firm's executives set the agenda. The meeting went on for two to three hours with nothing tangible being accomplished. The executive who set the agenda brought in spreadsheets that showed, unremarkably, that if we vastly increased our sales without increasing our expenses our profits would soar. There were some problems with the agenda that was set. At the time our business was going through a rough patch, was short on cash, and was bleeding cash. In addition, the projections, although technically correct, were wildly fanciful and had no basis in reality.

Things really went downhill when we got to the agenda item regarding executive compensation. The executive who drew up the agenda was in effect requesting a raise for himself. Part of the justification he was using for the raise was how well he ran meetings and how hard he worked setting the agenda! The compensation issue was, to say the least, divisive, since the company was hemorrhaging cash. It also wasn't relevant to the critical and time-sensitive issue at hand of sales, marketing, and product development planning. Once the ancillary, unnecessary, and divisive issue of executive compensation was raised, the meeting fell completely apart. It concluded with finger-pointing and resentment as the executives were blaming one another for the unfavorable position the business was in.

No decisions were reached and we continued to drift without a plan as to where to point the business. This drifting was causing us to lose large amounts of money and made the business's position even worse. The lesson we learned from this experience was very valuable: If you want (or need) to reach a consensus and conclusion, control the agenda and be very, very careful to avoid ancillary and unnecessary divisive issues. Now, whenever we have internal meetings where important decisions need to be made, one of the authors will personally set the agenda.

———

Here's another example. Many years ago, we got together with a group of physicians and other professionals to start a new certifying board for a certain physician specialty. Each of the persons involved in the negotiations to launch this board (including us) had their own issues and desires and some had potential conflicts of interest (we certainly did as we were interested in getting paid to train doctors before they became certified) in that they stood to make significant amounts of money from training fees, salaries, publications, consulting fees, and so on depending upon what was decided. We all got together on a conference call. No agenda was provided and nothing was decided. In fact, of the three hours of the call, ninety minutes were spent just trying to schedule the next call. We participated in several more unproductive calls like this.

We had a business to run and couldn't waste this much time herding cats. We suggested an in-person meeting and asked, "We will send out a proposed agenda, okay?" To sweeten the offer we suggested a resort location during high season. The doctors we were dealing with readily agreed to all three suggestions.

We set a tight hour-by-hour agenda. We ordered the agenda to get everyone to agree on an easy set of principles at the beginning. We took great pains to avoid unnecessary issues that could prove divisive or distracting. Our hour-by-hour specific agenda created mini deadlines for each of the many issues we were discussing. Whenever we started to fall behind on time someone would speed up the process by pointing out quite correctly the timelines on our agenda. The deadlines encouraged compromise. Not one person questioned the agenda, issues, order, or time to discuss each issue. We controlled the entire negotiation with a one-page agenda, which took thirty minutes to write and distribute.

The contrast with our previous unproductive conference telephone calls was astounding. In the one-day meeting, we resolved all the major outstanding issues. The board was founded and is operating to this day. It has trained and certified thousands of physicians and generated millions of dollars in economic activity. The board has raised the standard of practice in its area. We personally benefited from the board's existence as our firm was hired by the board to conduct training. Many other people in the room also benefited both financially and professionally. Without our asking "We will send out a proposed agenda, okay?" we don't know whether the board ever would have gotten off the ground.

Lesson

Taking on the task of writing and sending out the agenda can help you control the issues, timing, and momentum, and increase your chance of a favorable negotiation outcome. Asking "I will send out a proposed agenda, okay?" is the simple and low-key way to try to seize control of the agenda. When agendas are designed they should start with easy areas that likely will build confidence and rapport among the parties. Ancillary and unnecessary divisive issues should be avoided. To use the power of deadlines to maximum advantage, consider an agenda broken into specific time slots, each of which has its own implicit deadline.

How to Respond If You Are Asked
"I will send out a proposed agenda, okay?"

How you respond to this question depends upon what you want. If you would prefer that the other side prepare an agenda, then your answer should be a simple, "Yes, that would be helpful, thank you." If, on the other hand, you wish to control the agenda you can respond in various ways to try to seize for yourself the agenda making. For example, "I have already started one. I'll finish it ASAP and get it over to you" or "I can take care of that for you. I'll send one over shortly."

Question #9

WOULD YOU LIKE TO GET TOGETHER AND MEET IN PERSON?

On account of the time and expense of travel, parties are becoming less and less inclined to negotiate in person. Much of our modern negotiating takes place on the telephone or by e-mail. Although this may be more convenient, the results obtained from telephone and e-mail negotiations are often subpar. The reason for this is clear—telephone and e-mail negotiations often result in miscommunications because you can't see the expression on the other person's face or judge their tone correctly. Even more important, telephone and e-mail negotiations make it much harder to build strong person-to-person bonds with whomever you're negotiating with.

Simply asking whether the person you are negotiating with would like to get together in person with you can facilitate positive negotiation outcomes. If the person you are negotiating with agrees, it is our experience that there is much to be gained by negotiating in person. The advantages include:

- Taking the time to get to know the person and his likes, dislikes, interests, needs, and desires (i.e., what makes them tick).

- Bonding with the party you are negotiating with is much more effective when done in person.

- Being able to see the facial expressions of the other party can be extremely important. Is the party unconsciously nodding his assent . . . or shaking his head to indicate disagreement?

- Does the person you are negotiating with seem to be in a hurry, checking his watch, etc.? Or is he calm and relaxed and not seemingly under any time pressure?

- Body language can be extremely revealing to the observant negotiator. Is he saying one thing but his body language is sending a completely different message?

- How large is his negotiating file? Is it a large accordion file or a small folio with only ten to twenty pieces of paper? A large file indicates he is heavily invested in consummating a deal with you and won't readily let the deal slip away.

- How and when he takes notes can be revealing. Does he suddenly pick up his pen when one particular issue is raised?

When asked the question "Would you like to get together and meet in person?" the thought process the recipient goes through includes:

- Is this negotiation important enough for me to meet in person?

- Should I ask him to come to my office, go to his, or suggest a neutral site?

- How much time should we block out? Will one to two hours be sufficient or do we need an entire day or more?

- Is the chance of making progress at a face-to-face negotiation realistic enough to justify the time and expense of the meeting?

- If I decline to meet in person, what message am I sending and will this potentially jeopardize the negotiation?

Here are a couple of examples from our own experience where asking this simple question has completely turned around a poorly progressing negotiation.

Many years ago, we contacted a company that was an allied business. We sent a letter asking them if they would like to resell (distribute) the books that we publish to their clients and split the revenue with us 50-50. This was a very reasonable proposal as it would cost the allied company nothing and had the potential to generate substantial profits for them and us.

The reply came back: Sorry but we are not interested.

After waiting a few months the authors made a follow-up phone call and explained the benefits of the proposal.

The company rejected the proposal out of hand.

After several more rejections the authors called and asked, "Would you like to get together and meet in person?"

The recipient reluctantly agreed but asked us to travel 500 miles to their site.

We met the woman we'd approached for lunch at a nice country club. We discussed all types of things: Our children and her children. Our dogs and her dogs. The trials and tribulations of being a parent. The cost of colleges. What it was like to be a grandparent. The places that we had both traveled to. The lunch "meeting" went on for more than two hours. During the meeting the recipient mentioned in passing an out-of-print children's book she was trying to find as a gift for her grandchild—*The Land of Lost Buttons*. We talked about many other matters and had a fun and interesting lunch.

Upon returning to the office, we were asked, "Did you get the deal?" Our partner was incredulous when we told him that we never talked business with the woman.

"You mean to tell me that you spent an entire day and $600 in airfare and never discussed business? That is unbelievable!" he replied.

We informed our partner that if he wanted a deal he needed to do only one thing—find us a copy of a book that has been out of print for thirty years, *The Land of Lost Buttons*!

The book was located and mailed to our lunch partner with a note that read: "The difficult we do routinely, the impossible takes a little longer." A few days later we received a tearful phone call from the recipient telling us it was the nicest thing anyone has ever done for her. Shortly thereafter we received a second phone call saying that the recipient ran interference for us at the company and that they would begin to resell our books forthwith. This business relationship has continued to this day and has resulted in significant profits for both companies.

More recently, we were starting to have concerns about a vendor we had been using for a few years. We had recently expanded our business dealings and they were now doing customized Web site design work for us. We hired them to redo our company's main Web site and e-commerce platforms, which is a significant job. Unfortunately, the project immediately fell sharply behind schedule. Worse, our new contact at the company would not return our phone calls as he was swamped with other work and personal problems. We became frustrated and angry. The level of service we were receiving was unacceptable.

In sum, our relationship was pushed to the breaking point. We were contemplating firing them. This would be a serious step, as it would further delay the launch of our new Web site. On the other hand, we couldn't go on with such poor customer service. We realized that e-mail or the phone would be a very poor medium for communicating how we felt. We sent an e-mail and asked if we could get together in person. They agreed.

At the meeting we looked the owner in the eye and explained the situation. We praised their past work. We empathized with his personal problems, but we clearly stated what we expected in terms of service: timely work and calls back when requested. Our contact pleaded guilty and thanked us profusely for coming in to see him. He said we would never have these problems again and we never have. The in-person meeting requested by us saved both parties a lot of time and money.

You may ask, "What happens if the person you are negotiating with responds that they won't get together in person?" The short answer is, "Usually nothing bad." If they won't grant you the courtesy of a meeting, this can help you identify people whom you might not want to be dealing with in the first case and who are not really committed to the project. If they have a legitimate reason for not being able to get together in person, there was certainly no harm in asking.

Lesson

When things are going poorly, ask for an in-person meeting. Negotiating in person can dramatically change the course of negotiations to mutual advantage.

How to Respond If You Are Asked "Would you like to get together and meet in person?"

If you want to make a deal and would like to create a long-term relationship, this question should be answered in the affirmative. Of course, if you don't feel as though you need a deal and would like to increase your bargaining power, you can also answer the question with conditions. For example, "Please send me over a list of what you would like to accomplish at the meeting and also provide me a report on the lowest pricing you have ever provided any customer. After I have reviewed these and if they meet my approval I will consider meeting with you here in my office."

You will tend to get a lot of requests for in-person meetings from salespeople. Good salespeople always want to meet in person because they realize it is tougher to say "no" to someone in person. A good way to deal with a salesperson requesting such a meeting that you really don't want is to either just say "no" or to request some type of perk. For example, "Yes, I'd love to talk to you in person. If you can comp my wife and me for a weekend at your hotel, we can meet for a few minutes on Sunday morning." Alternatively, "Thanks for the call, Charlie. My schedule is too crazy to get together with you just now. If you have any more Red Sox tickets available for your clients, please let me know. My son loved it the last time you comped us." You could also respond something like, "I assume that if we met, you would be bringing free samples with you?"

Question #10

CAN WE AGREE TO PUT THE PAST BEHIND US AND DISCUSS ONLY THE FUTURE?

Let's face it, many times we need to negotiate with people with whom we've had strained relations in the past. Oftentimes, both parties have numerous grievances concerning injustices that they believe they were subjected to in the past at the hands of the other party. Such a history in many cases makes the ongoing negotiations extremely difficult. A good example of this is, of course, the Israeli-Palestinian conflict. This situation may also commonly occur in troubled marriages or business relationships gone sour. "Can we agree to put the past behind us and discuss only the future?" can be used to break free of the past in just such situations. This question is designed to:

- Have both sides avoid an incessant rehashing of the past.

- Avoid a point-by-point review of old outstanding issues that have little or no relevance to the current negotiation.

- Ask for a vote of confidence, for example, that despite past difficulties, a new agreement is desirable/possible.

- Act as a tacit trial balloon. It is implicit that the person asking the question would be willing to discuss only the future if the other party would agree to this approach.

- Obtain at least a partial buy-in for a potential new agreement. The very fact that someone would agree to this strongly suggests that they are seriously interested in reaching an agreement and moving forward.

What is implicit in this question is very powerful—namely, that if the parties don't agree to put the past behind them, there will be no successful negotiation or agreement in the present. While the question is not presented as a take-it-or-leave-it scenario (that is not explicitly stated), the implication is clear enough. If the parties continue to argue about the past, they realistically cannot and will not make any progress in this negotiation.

As you can see from the Palestinian-Israeli conflict, some conflicts will never be resolved if the parties focus on the past. When involved in a negotiation where you have a long and hostile history with the person you are negotiating with, this is a great win-win question to ask. If the answer comes back that the person you are negotiating with is not ready to discuss only the future, you have won in that you have a pretty clear indication that it may be a waste of time to continue negotiating. If the answer comes back in the affirmative, however, you have learned that it's possible to reach a mutually satisfying agreement.

We ourselves have used this approach when negotiating with problem employees. For several years we had to deal with a very talented employee who was creating havoc at our office. The complaints from co-employees kept mounting. We were reluctant to let the employee go because his unique talents and skills were valuable to us. Meeting with the employee to discuss the problems just resulted in a rehashing of past problems and him feeling perceived slights by co-employees and management. When we were near the end of our rope we took a different approach. We asked him, "Can we agree to put the past behind us and discuss only the future?" He smiled, relieved that he was not being let go, and asked, "What can I do to avoid future problems and become a more valuable employee?" This one question helped us all to put the past behind us and concentrate on the future. The turnaround in his performance was dramatic and very positive.

This can also be a great question to use in nonbusiness situations. Here's an example. A good friend of ours, whom we'll call Jerry, was having trouble with his marriage. His wife (we'll call her Janice) had asked Jerry to move out mainly because of issues dealing with his breadwinning and helping out with the family. There were no questions of infidelity, drug use, or anything like that. Jerry was heartbroken. Jerry loved his wife and two beautiful young children very much. His sole purpose in life became getting his family back.

For the next few months, Jerry kept asking Janice if he could move back home. The results were always the same. Janice would bring up the issues of the past and the conversation would deteriorate from there. We kept checking in with Jerry to see how he was getting along. Jerry started getting depressed. He quit his job. Soon he began to not return our calls and e-mails. Finally, one day, we called Jerry and left a voice message (he wouldn't pick up the phone) that said, "We have an idea how you can get Janice back. Call us if you're interested."

The phone rang about five minutes later and it was Jerry. "How can I do it?" he asked anxiously. We explained that nothing positive would ever happen as long as he and Janice kept rehashing the past. If he wanted to find out if she really wanted him back, he should ask her, "Can we agree to put the past behind us and discuss only the future?" Jerry was very, very appreciative of our advice. It sounded like he was totally reinvigorated at finally having a way out of the destructive loop he was in with Janice.

Always keep in mind that more than one of the questions we explain in this book can, and often should, be used to help you in a particular negotiation you are involved in. For example, "Can we put the past behind us?" has been part of some of the other negotiations described elsewhere in this book. Consider how this question helped greatly facilitate the situations described below when used in conjunction with the questions "Can we meet in person?" and "Can we agree to stay here until we reach an agreement?"

Many years ago, we invited a friend into a business partnership with us. To make a long story short, the arrangement didn't work out well. The profitability of the partnership wasn't as great as we all had hoped and our friend, who was in debt, had many obligations and was in a difficult situation. He was very unhappy because he wasn't making as much money as he needed to support his family in the lifestyle he desired. He stopped working with us to take outside employment but still held his ownership in the partnership. The partnership continued to drain cash and this made matters, to say the least, very tense. Things deteriorated rapidly. Soon, we weren't talking at all. Then, on almost a weekly basis, we started to receive threatening letters from our friend demanding that we pay him large amounts of money. This went on for many months. We started to think about getting a lawyer.

When feelings are passionate, negotiating via the phone or e-mail is not preferred. In light of this, we decided to arrange an in-person meeting with our friend. We met and greeted each other politely. The tension was palpable as we shook hands. As soon as we sat down, we asked our friend one question, "Can we agree to put the past behind us and discuss only the future?" The answer came back in the affirmative and you could see the hostility melt away from all of us. Within thirty minutes, we were able to agree on terms to buy him out of his interest in the partnership. This was mutually beneficial financially to all of us. More important, we were able to get our friendship back on track. We remain friends to this day.

More recently, we were involved in a rapidly deteriorating relationship with one of our information technology vendors who was creating a new Web site for our company. The vendor had been experiencing many personal and professional problems. One of the vendor's partners left and this was a major distraction for the vendor. Then the vendor's sibling came down with a major health problem.

We decided to arrange a face-to-face meeting. At the meeting we purposefully avoided going over the past and rehashing all the failures of the vendor. Instead, as soon as we sat down, we asked, "Can we agree to put the past behind us and discuss only the future?" The answer came back, "I am very grateful for that." The tension in the room evaporated. We were no longer frustrated clients but three professionals working together to problem solve. The meeting went very positively. We have had greatly improved service ever since that day.

Lesson

The question "Can we agree to put the past behind us and discuss only the future?" can be extremely effective in helping reach an agreement in a case where there is bad blood between the parties. Putting the parties' past differences behind them in one fell swoop is a shrewd, effective, and proven negotiating strategy.

How to Respond If You Are Asked "Can we agree to put the past behind us and discuss only the future?"

If you want to reach an agreement with someone you have bad blood with, the best answer to this question is usually "Yes, I think that would be very helpful." Such an answer implies that you realize that rehashing past grievances is not productive and that you would like to move on. Rejecting the proposition in this question may feel good, but you will be much less likely to come to a constructive resolution.

Question #11

ARE YOU A TEAM PLAYER?

"Are you a team player?" is an excellent question to ask when you are dealing with someone in an employer/employee-type relationship who is asking for greater benefits than you wish to or are able to pay. This question is best deployed either preemptively or in response to a demand beyond what you are willing to offer. It can often be very effective in encouraging the person you are working with not to make big demands (when used preemptively) or back off of previously made demands (when used in response to a demand).

The subtexts of "Are you a team player?" are clear and powerful. These are: We're all in this together. We need team players. Team players are cooperative and considerate and don't make trouble.

"Are you a team player?" is a very low-risk question. What could be more harmless than asking someone whether or not they are a team player? Since there is little to no risk to the question it can be used routinely when dealing with long-term employer/employee-type situations.

What's more, the question is extremely effective. It is worded in such a way that the answer you will almost invariably receive to it is "yes." Indeed, how could the answer be anything other than "yes," or "of course"? Any other answer could be suicidal. Once the person you are negotiating with is prompted to state that he is a team player, your negotiation position will be greatly improved. To support your argument as to why you cannot give the person what he is demanding, all you need to do is point to the financial, organizational, social, and other needs of the team.

As mentioned above, one way to use this question is preemptively, that is, to use it before you receive a demand from the person you are negotiating with. For example:

EMPLOYER: I would like to offer you the position, but before I do, I'd like to ask you one more critical question.

POTENTIAL EMPLOYEE: Shoot.

EMPLOYER: Are you a team player?

POTENTIAL EMPLOYEE: Absolutely.

EMPLOYER: I'm so glad to hear that. This company is a team. Different people play different positions. We all support each other with the goal of having the company succeed. You understand that?

POTENTIAL EMPLOYEE: Yes, of course.

EMPLOYER: Okay, I'd like to formally offer you the position. The salary for your entry-level position is $32,000 a year. If you do your job and help the team succeed, you will have ample opportunities for bonuses, profit sharing, and advancement. When would you like to start?

POTENTIAL EMPLOYEE: Ummm, I was hoping for a little more. Can I negotiate the salary?

EMPLOYER: Let me be frank here. We are looking for team players who are going to focus on what they can do for the team, not the other way around. We do not want people here who are primarily concerned with what we can do for them and who ask for raises all the time. Are we on the same page?

POTENTIAL EMPLOYEE: $32,000 will be fine. I can start on Monday.

EMPLOYER: Great. We look forward to it.

The preemptive use of the "Are you a team player?" helped set the stage for the salary negotiations that followed. Once the potential employee agreed to being a team player he handed the employer ammunition to use against him. This ammunition was effectively used by the employer, and the prospective employee was unable to negotiate an increase in starting salary.

We often use this question in response to extraordinary employee demands. We usually take a hard line with such demands since meeting these demands can cause a host of financial and office politics problems. Let's take a look at an example where "Are you a team player?" is used to respond to a demand an employer like the authors has received.

EMPLOYEE: Thanks for meeting with me, Steve. I wanted to discuss compensation. I work very hard for you here and am doing a great job. I think I deserve a $20,000 raise. I'm worth it.

AUTHOR (EMPLOYER): Your review is at the end of April; you can certainly expect an adjustment then.

EMPLOYEE: I've got bills to pay. Student loans. With all I do here, I am worth another $20,000, starting immediately.

AUTHOR (EMPLOYER): Are you a team player?

EMPLOYEE: Of course.

AUTHOR (EMPLOYER): You're a friend, Charlie, so I will be frank. We don't need people who merely say they are team players. We need people who *act* like loyal team players. Loyal team players don't ask for special treatment, extraordinary compensation, or unscheduled raises. Loyal team members do their jobs, wait their turn, and don't make waves. If I were to do this for you it could cause major resentment with the other team members. Besides that, the organization can't afford to pay what you are looking for and I need to look out for the organization as a whole. Your review is in April. After your review you can expect to get a salary adjustment in line with your position and in line with the adjustments the other team members will receive. If this is a problem, please let me know now. If not, I'll show you the courtesy of forgetting we had this conversation and will look forward to sitting down with you for your review in April.

EMPLOYEE: Okay, I appreciate that, Steve. Let's talk again in April.

In the above example, the "Are you a team player?" question was used effectively to set up the employer's argument. The employee, as can be expected, agreed that he was a team player. This allowed the employer to make a very effective argument as to why the employee's demand could not be acceded to.

Lesson

"Are you a team player?" can be a very effective question when negotiating with an employee. "Are you a team player?" is low risk and can be used either preemptively or in response to a demand from an employee. The answer you receive to this question will almost always be in the affirmative. Once you have received a positive response, you can use this response to bolster your negotiating position by pointing out why what the employee is asking for is not what a team player would do.

How to Respond If You Are Asked "Are you a team player?"

"Are you a team player?" is a question that really must be answered in the affirmative. That said, the best way to answer this is probably with a qualifier. For example, "Yes, but I assume you don't want an unhappy member on your team?" Here the implicit message is simple. I am a team player, but what you are suggesting does not make me happy and needs to be sweetened to make this work for both of us.

PART IV

Anchors

INTRODUCTION: One sophisticated negotiating tactic is called anchoring. Anchoring basically involves setting the ballpark that the negotiation starts from. This ballpark could be a proposed price or other terms. The advantage of successfully anchoring the other party is that they are then forced to negotiate in a designated area and from a favorable position proposed by you. This part contains questions that you can use to attempt to anchor the other party.

Question #12

CAN YOU DO THE JOB FOR $X?

Most negotiators believe that it is always a good strategy to get the person you are negotiating with to name his price to start the negotiation. We don't. The reasons other negotiators believe you should let the person you are negotiating with name the first price may include:

- **The person may theoretically name a price lower than one you would offer (this is rarely true).**

- **Getting the person to name his price will let you negotiate the price down.**

- **How high the person goes will let you gauge:**
    - **how eager they are to reach an agreement**
    - **if they are an experienced negotiator**
    - **if they are realistic or if they have wild expectations**
    - **how likely you are to be able to reach an agreement with the recipient**

There are many problems with the negotiation strategy of getting your opponent to name his price. These problems include:

- Encouraging the recipient to compute how much he is worth

- Forcing the recipient to come up with an inflated price to leave himself room to negotiate

- Giving the person time to think about the question

- Raising their expectations and desires

In our opinion, once a person arrives at a figure he will *never* be satisfied with the lower figure you negotiate. Each dollar less he will receive is viewed as a "dollar lost." Getting the person to move off of his number can be difficult and fraught with resistance and resentment.

Our take on price naming is not mainstream, but we firmly believe in it. We believe in "anchoring" the person you are negotiating with to a price you first suggest. The way this is done is by asking a simple question such as "Can you do the job for $3,000?"

The thought process the recipient of this question will go through is as follows:

a. At least I have a ballpark price.
b. The price is too low.
c. If that is their opening offer, I can get more.
d. I will ask for more but not too much more as I don't want to be unrealistic.
e. If I get more I will be a hero and a superior negotiator.

By asking the question, *you* have set the parameters for the price. The recipient will almost always stay in this ballpark when asking for more. The person you are negotiating with has in effect become anchored to your number and won't be able to drift too far away from it. All subsequent negotiating then proceeds from your original number. This is a tremendous advantage.

We have used and continue to use this technique in our business. When we invite speakers to speak for us at our national conferences we tell them up front that we cannot pay an honorarium. They are then anchored to this concept and ask only for marginal items such as an extra night in the hotel, a rental car, or a discount on a product we sell. Consider the alternative if we asked the speaker what they usually get for speaking. The answer could be thousands of dollars. We'd *never* get them off that figure down to zero. We'd then be anchored to *their* number.

When we practiced law, we'd use this question all the time to anchor a defense attorney to our settlement demand. "Can you settle the case for "$100,000?" we would ask. That's the starting point of the negotiation. If he gets us down to $50,000, he looks like a hero and feels great. We knew the case was worth only $35,000, so we're happy, too.

Let's look at one final example. We were hiring an expert to write and star in an education video we were producing. Here's how the negotiation went:

> **AUTHORS:** We would like you to be the content expert on a video we are shooting. We know you are the leader in the field. It will be a thirty-minute video. The good news is that we can film right at your office and you will be helping out many people.
> **EXPERT:** Thank you for the kind words. A thirty-minute video doesn't sound too bad. Will I be compensated?
> **AUTHORS:** Well, we don't normally pay due to the publicity generated, but in your case we can make an exception. Can you do the job for $3,000?

EXPERT: Well, I would love to do it but . . . I have two kids in college. I can't do it . . . for less than . . . $6,000?

AUTHORS: Well, that's a lot more than we had planned but . . . let me make a call, hold on a minute. . . . (After a few minutes.) Okay, you got it, $6,000.

EXPERT: Great! When do we start?

What has happened here? The recipient went through the process outlined above and demanded twice what was offered. He had little time to think this question through. He is very pleased with himself and his negotiating prowess. He was "anchored" to the $3,000 price and the most he thought he could get away with asking is *twice* that, $6,000. We controlled the situation by asking if he could do the work for our price.

In fact had he not been anchored to our price he would have and should have considered:

- How much does he normally make per hour?

- How many hours will it take to film the video (note it is not thirty minutes and will be closer to eight hours)?

- Will the company be selling the video? At what price? How many will they likely sell?

- Will he also have to write the script? (Yes. He is the expert.)

Lesson

Asking the simple question "Can you do it for $X?" quietly anchors the person you are negotiating with to *your* price and puts you in control of the ballpark that the final price will be.

As above, once the recipient has named the price, he is in no position to complain about the $6,000 agreed to. It is his price! You gave him exactly what he asked for, but you limited him to the general parameters of the price in your question.

How to Respond If You Are Asked "Can you do it for $X?"

There are different ways to respond to this question. If you have a perfect understanding of what the job entails and how much it is worth to you, and if the offer you received was ridiculously low, you can and should come back with a price of your own *without any thought whatsoever to the figure you were presented with.* This ignores the person's attempt to anchor you and instead attempts to anchor them to *your* number. For example, "No, my fee for speaking is $10,000 a day." Since you were being offered a lousy deal, there is no risk in this approach.

Alternatively, if you don't have a good understanding of what exactly you are being asked to do, the best response is to find out. For example, you could respond, "We're nowhere near the point where we can discuss money. Please send me the exact specs of what you are looking for and I will get back to you with any questions I have. After I have a complete understanding, I would be pleased to provide you with our price." The above response completely disregards their attempt to anchor you and helps you determine the critical information of exactly what you are being asked to do.

Question #13

WHAT IS THE MOST YOU HAVE EVER PAID FOR THIS SERVICE OR PRODUCT?

This is a great question for a seller to ask a potential buyer. At first glance, this question seems so simplistic and direct that it's almost hard to believe it works. Take it from us, though—we've used it time and again. It is simple and it works. What makes this question successful? The question is artfully phrased to shock the recipient and make him or her quite concerned about answering truthfully and not obfuscating the truth. What if he or she were to lie or try to obfuscate the truth? The problems with responding dishonestly are numerous:

- The lie or evasion may be painfully obvious.

- If you are caught in a lie, any trust or goodwill may be permanently damaged, and the entire deal can be lost.

- If the deal the parties are working on involves an ongoing relationship, lying or being evasive can

damage trust and credibility, and call into question whether this is the type of person/company/organization one would want to do business with in the long term.

So, telling the truth—no matter how painful or expensive—may be the single best and most absolute way to cement a long-term relationship. The question works so effectively because it assumes that the prospective buyer *will* pay you this "most ever paid" amount. Any experienced negotiator knows and understands that once the number is out there it will be difficult or impossible to take it back.

Consider the following example from our own experiences. As previously mentioned, the authors were retained as professional negotiators to assist a leading, well-respected medical journal to negotiate a better deal with their publishing company. The non-profit medical society that owned all the rights to the journal felt that they were being substantially shortchanged by their publishing company in terms of how much the publishing company was compensating them. This turned out to be true. After much discussion an RFP (request for proposal) was sent out to the leading medical publishing companies worldwide. This RFP formally invited publishers to compete for the journal's business and, in effect, put the contract out to bid.

Many companies responded, and after a lengthy winnowing-down process, the number of publishers in the running was reduced to three. These three were all invited to a final meeting during which the journal would choose the winning bidder. In an all-day session, lengthy PowerPoint presentations were made to the society by each of the three publishers. The society eventually narrowed the list further and decided on their first choice. A new date was chosen for a full day of negotiation with the society's publisher of choice.

During the first five hours of the negotiation with their top choice, the society *never* talked about money. A list of twenty-seven items dealing with processes, quality control, culture, permissions, past articles, book conversions, and other issues was presented, and one by one the publisher acquiesced to all of them. It eventually became clear that the publisher was extremely invested in landing this journal. They freely admitted it would be the jewel in their crown, and that they were going to use this acquisition to attract other journals. Once we began talking financials, many of the society's financial terms were quickly agreed to, including royalty rate, royalty frequencies, and payment for editorial support. The question of a signing bonus (which the society had never requested previously) and an annual inflation escalator clause for the society remained to be negotiated.

During a much-needed break, the author and lead negotiator for the society asked to talk to the lead negotiator for the publisher in the hallway away from all the other parties.

We asked the single question "What is the most you have ever paid in acquiring any one of your hundreds of journals?"

After blinking and wincing slightly, the publisher replied with a signing bonus and annual inflation escalator clause that we never even dreamed of asking for. We asked for similar treatment and the publisher agreed. This single question and response resulted in *millions* of additional dollars being paid to the society. All parties were satisfied. Think about it. One question worth millions of dollars. That's the power of asking the right question in a negotiation.

Lesson

Asking, "What is the most you have ever paid for this service or product?" dramatically and positively influenced the outcome of our negotiation. You can use the same question, tailored to your specific negotiation scenario, to equally dramatic and beneficial effect. (Note: If you are the buyer, you can use the question "What's the least amount of money you have ever sold one of these for?" to equal effect.)

How to Respond If You Are Asked
"What is the most you have ever paid for
this service or product?"

There are many different ways to deal with this question if you are asked it. The first way involves disputing the very premise of the question that you have bought or sold *this exact* item before. In this case your response is a simple "Well, we never have before. This is different than what we've done in the past." When using this approach you will, of course, need to be prepared if pressed to explain why this situation is different. Another variation of this approach is to push back with something like, "What happened before the stock market crash and the market fell out is certainly in no way relevant to what we have before us today."

Another way to deal with this question is to claim ignorance. A simple "I don't know" or "I don't believe we keep records on that" could suffice.

Finally, you can also take a direct approach to such a direct question. A simple direct answer could be, "I am sorry but we don't discuss proprietary information" or "We do not release other clients' financial information."

Question #14

CAN YOU GIVE ME A BALLPARK FIGURE FOR YOUR PRODUCTS OR SERVICE?

"Can you give me a ballpark figure for your products or service?" is used to catch a seller off guard. The hope is that the seller will throw out a low price so as not to lose a chance at your business. Even if the ballpark price is later subject to negotiation, the seller will in essence be anchored to the low ballpark price in future negotiations.

The subtext of the question is easily recognizable to the seller. Price is important to you and you are shopping around for the lowest price. When hearing this question the seller will be highly motivated to leave you with a low, appealing price. To do otherwise would leave the seller in a situation where he may lose the deal altogether.

"Can you give me a ballpark figure for your products or service?" is most appropriately asked when buying a customized service such as consulting, professional services (legal, accounting, etc.), or construction, where the scope of work is difficult to determine without significantly more research by the seller. This question is not appropriate where the scope of the product or services is clear and the seller is advertising a price.

The best time to ask this question is at the very beginning of an inquiry with a potential seller. It also can be helpful to slip into your delivery that you are shopping around. For example, "Hi, I'm looking into an irrigation system for my house and am calling a few vendors. Can you give me a ballpark price on a system for my house?" The earlier in the inquiry you ask this question, the more the seller will be caught off guard.

Asking for a ballpark price has the added advantage of being low risk. The response you are most likely to get is a request for further details or the ballpark price you were looking for. In either situation, you have lost nothing by merely asking for a ballpark price. All your options remain open.

If you are pressed by the seller for more details you will have a decision to make. The more details you provide, the less likely the seller is to hastily quote a price that is very favorably low. However, if you refuse to provide details, the seller will often refuse to provide a ballpark price—since he doesn't really know what he is quoting out. If you then continue to press on the ballpark price you may lose the advantage of getting a bid from this particular seller. There is real risk in this since the more options you have, the better deal you will get.

If you make the decision to press for a ballpark price we recommend the following. First, have a ready excuse in hand as to why you need a ballpark price. For example, "I don't want to go through a long discussion and waste everyone's time if you're not in our ballpark." Another good technique is to claim ignorance. For example, "I don't have all the details you are looking for; my boss just told me to call and find out how much it would cost." Finally, to reduce your risk, always leave yourself some wiggle room. Never paint yourself into a corner by saying with absolute certainty that you require a ballpark price to continue exploring a purchase.

The eventual response that you are looking for is, of course, a ballpark price. Since the seller presumably wants your business, this is likely to be a tempting price. If it's a high price you can move on to competing sellers and you have saved the time you might have wasted having an uncompetitive seller prepare a detailed quote. If the ballpark price comes back very competitive you can and should point back to this price in all future negotiations with each and every vendor you are talking to.

A physician we know had this ballpark question used against him a few years ago. He was called up to give a talk to a group of people from the insurance industry. Here's about how the negotiation went:

> **MEETING REPRESENTATIVE:** Doctor, we would like you to come and speak to our group—it's a one-day assignment on March 4th in Miami. Could you give me a ballpark figure of your charges, including travel?
> **PHYSICIAN:** Sure, one day plus travel . . . would $5,000 fit your budget?
> **MEETING REPRESENTATION:** Well, it's a little more than we hoped to pay, but call it $5,000 all-inclusive.
> **PHYSICIAN:** Thank you.

The physician in this real-life example later found out that the insurance company was charging a $300 registration fee to the event where he was the only speaker. Approximately 300 people came to the event. The event generated $90,000 and he was paid only $5,000, including expenses. This was a direct result of his mistake in rushing to quote a price without knowing all the important details of what he was being asked to do.

Here's another example. Recently, our office was looking for a piece of specialized office equipment. We found out through our research that three competing companies made these machines. There were no prices for these listed anywhere, however. You had to call the sales department. We had one of our employees use this technique for us. Two of the companies refused to give a ballpark price since there were many options, variables, and service plans to consider. Here's about how it went with one of the companies we called, however:

> **AUTHORS' EMPLOYEE:** Hi, I am researching your XYZ123 machine. Can you give me a ballpark price on that?
>
> **SALESPERSON:** I can help you with that. First of all, how are you doing?
>
> **AUTHORS' EMPLOYEE:** Excellent, and you?
>
> **SALESPERSON:** Great, thanks. Can I ask you some questions?
>
> **AUTHORS' EMPLOYEE:** Actually no. My boss gave me a big list of vendors to contact and he told me not to get bogged down with the salespeople, just to get a ballpark price to see if it's something we could consider. I am very sorry about this. He's kind of particular, my boss is. I only have an hour to get through a big list here. Can you give me that ballpark?
>
> **SALESPERSON:** $5,000.
>
> **AUTHORS' EMPLOYEE:** Thanks, we'll get back to you.

Any decent salesperson knows that if someone is obviously shopping around they will want to leave the potential buyer with an attractive price. This is exactly what the salesperson did here. Our employee was well prepared to fend off requests for details and our gambit worked. He was also well prepared to reinforce the message that price was critically important to us and that we were shopping around. We later took the $5,000 figure and later used it against *all three vendors* in the more detailed negotiations that followed and ended up purchasing the equipment on very favorable terms.

Lesson

"Can you give me a ballpark figure for your products or service?" is most appropriately used when buying consulting, construction, professional services, and other customized services. Asking for a ballpark price can be effective as it usually catches the recipient off guard and leads to an excellent anchor price. If and when the person you are negotiating with tries to move away from this anchor price you can effectively point back to the quoted ballpark price. "Can you give me a ballpark figure for your products or service?" is low risk as long as you leave yourself an out. To have the best chance of this question working, you should be prepared to provide a rationale as to why you don't want a detailed quote. This question is best deployed as early as possible in a negotiation.

How to Respond If You Are Asked "Can you give me a ballpark figure for your products or service?"

Giving a ballpark price where you don't know the exact details is a loser for a seller and should be assiduously avoided. The response to this question should be a firm "I can actually do much better than that. I'd be happy to give you a precise written quote, but I'd need to get some more information from you. It will only take around five minutes and we can do it right over the phone now." This sample response is eminently reasonable since you offer to give them even more than what they were asking for—a firm, written price instead of a ballpark price.

Question #15

ARE YOU AWARE OF THE INDUSTRY STANDARDS HERE?

This question is designed to get the person you are negotiating with to agree to make the standards the starting point of the negotiation. A prerequisite for successful use of this question is to research carefully what the industry standards are.

The question is well designed in that it implies that you're intimately familiar with what the industry standards are. This would tend to indicate that you are well informed and will not be easily taken advantage of in a negotiation. It is also well designed in that it is very difficult for the person you are negotiating with to later offer you substandard terms without his knowing that he would be running a strong risk of potentially alienating you.

Let's take a look at an example from our experiences where we've successfully used the question "Are you aware of the industry standards here?"

———

The authors have written several textbooks for many major publishers. Here is how one of our negotiations with one of those major publishers went:

> **PUBLISHER:** We would like you to write a textbook for us.
> **AUTHORS:** That sounds interesting. What are the terms?
> **PUBLISHER:** Oh, we provide the standard 10 percent royalty.
> **AUTHORS:** Are you aware of the industry standards here? These contracts usually pay 15 percent.
> **PUBLISHER:** Well, there is a range.... Ten to 15 percent is standard, yes.
> **AUTHOR:** How much time and effort do you spend getting manuscripts in on time, editing, rewriting, before they are ready to publish?
> **PUBLISHER:** The short answer ... too much.
> **AUTHOR:** We guarantee that our book will be in on time and ready to publish. We are professional writers and have already written ten textbooks.
> **PUBLISHER:** That would be very unusual.
> **AUTHOR:** We are unusual people and we deserve the highest royalty, 15 percent.
> **PUBLISHER:** Let me check with my superiors.

The publisher called back a couple of days later and agreed to our 15 percent demand. Using industry standards allowed us to increase our royalty rate by 50 percent. Doing our homework to research this and asking the right question at the right time really paid off for us.

There have been many other times where we have used industry standards to move terms in a more favorable direction. One common example is when we negotiate contracts with hotels to hold our meetings. Whenever we see something out of the ordinary and to our disadvantage in one of these contracts, we always ask, "Are you aware of the industry standards here?" This simple question almost always results in a noxious clause or term being removed, and in an improvement of terms that brings them more in line with industry standards.

Lesson

"Are you aware of the industry standards here?" can be a very effective negotiating question provided that you have done your homework on what the industry standards are. The use of this question can help assure that you don't end up with an unusually poor deal.

How to Respond If You Are Asked "Are you aware of the industry standards here?"

There are two different general ways to respond to this question. The first is to dispute that there actually are governing industry standards in this particular case. The key here is to distinguish your situation and explain why the industry standards are not pertinent. For example, "I am aware of the industry standards for publishing in general, certainly, but this situation is different. Let me explain why. . . ."

The alternative way to respond to this question is to be well prepared to use the standards to your own advantage. Here you would want to point out how the standards benefit you. What you are in effect stating is that you are aware of the standards, here is what they are, and let's go ahead and use them as they favor me not you. For example, "Yes, the industry standard is no more than 10 percent royalty." Note that such a response requires you knowing your stuff and doing your homework.

PART V

Power Tools

INTRODUCTION: Negotiating success is directly related to how much negotiating power you can develop. Negotiating power is generated by techniques such as demonstrating what the other party has to lose, limiting the other party's alternatives, developing your own alternatives, not appearing overeager, dangling the possibility of future work in front of the other party, and disclosing information that credibly shows why you cannot agree to the other party's proposed terms. The questions in this part are designed to help you harness and generate negotiating power.

Question #16

ARE YOU PREPARED TO LOSE US AS A CUSTOMER TODAY?

As a good, long-term customer of a product or service, you are frequently in an excellent position to negotiate better pricing for a continuation of that product or service. When striking such a deal, a gently toned asking of "Are you prepared to lose us as a customer today?" can be extremely effective in wringing the best possible terms out of the product or service provider.

To use this question effectively, you must do the preparation work of gaining the reputation of being a good customer with the provider. What makes for a "good" long-term customer?

- A customer who pays his bills promptly without delay, complaints, or nickel-and-diming the provider

- One who has been with the provider/vendor for an extended period of time

- One who has a continuing need for a product/service

- Efficient customers who are organized and know what they want

- Customers who are happy to refer other potential customers

Existing customers are far more profitable than new customers since it can be hugely expensive and quite difficult to acquire a new customer. When faced with the question "Are you prepared to lose us as a customer today?" the company's salesperson or representative is confronted with many difficult issues:

- His job is to win and not lose business.

- His compensation may be directly tied to keeping you as a customer through a commission.

- If the customer is lost he will have to explain this in detail and probably at great length to his superiors.

- It may be up to him to replace this customer with another one of similar quality—which is no easy task.

- He will have to calculate:
    — the short-term and long-term value to the company of this customer
    — how much profit will be lost if the customer moves on
    — how this profit will be replaced
    — how much less profit his company will take in order to retain this good customer

Most salespeople and representatives are well aware of the daunting task of replacing a good customer. The cost of acquiring new customers ranges from six times to as high as thirteen times the cost of servicing existing ones.

With this in mind, salespeople and company representatives will bend over backward to find ways to keep good customers happy and retain them.

The best way to use this question is first to build a reputation as a good customer as we have described above. If you are a pain in the neck, the vendor will probably be happy to get rid of you. Second, do your homework and get lower competing bids. Finally, when you ask, ask nicely and not in a threatening manner. Justify your actions as economic necessity. Remember that you'll need to work with this vendor in the future and they have to make a profit, too, so don't be unreasonable if you want to keep them as a vendor.

We have used this question and approach numerous times. Our company, SEAK, Inc., was greatly affected by the sudden economic downturn that started in the fall of 2008. The vast majority of our revenues come from consulting and training. In a sharp downturn like the one we experienced, the first thing most companies cut back on is consulting and training. Needless to say, this put us in a challenging business position.

To promote our conferences and consulting, we mail more than a million multicolored thirty-six-page brochures each year. These cost hundreds of thousands of dollars to print. We have used a particular printer to print these for many years. Their quality has been continuously excellent. This is a prime concern of ours since these color brochures are responsible for a large portion of our income.

When the financial crisis of 2008 came along, we had no choice but to save money wherever possible. Because our printer's quality was so good, and their customer service was superb, we wanted to stay with them. It was time to renegotiate a better deal.

Part of our negotiating preparation had already been done. We were a good customer . . . no, we were a *great* customer. We paid our bills on time, every time. We came back year after year. We were easy to deal with. We never asked for freebies like sports tickets or gifts or anything like that (which many vendors use to try to suck up to customers).

The next part of our preparation took some work. We instructed one of our associates to search high and low and get us a better price from other printing companies on the types of brochures we print. It took him about a month, but he did. The vast majority of the quotes he received were higher than what we were currently paying. He did find some significantly lower ones, however. With these quotes in hand, we began negotiating. Here's how it went:

AUTHORS: John, I assume you received that quote from your competitor that we sent over?

PRINTER: Yes, we did. Thank you for that.

AUTHORS: You know we're looking for you to beat that?

PRINTER: Yes, I realize that. They are in the middle of nowhere. Our costs are higher than theirs.

AUTHOR: I understand that. You guys have been great to us. We think you do very nice work. The customer service has been superb. We really want to stay with you, but with the current downturn we are under tremendous financial pressure. Before I go with them, I just wanted to give you the courtesy of a phone call and ask you directly: Are prepared to lose us as a customer today?

PRINTER: I appreciate the opportunity. Give me twenty-four hours and let me see what we can come up with.

The next day we heard back from them. The printer agreed to meet 80 percent of the difference in price. They said they couldn't go any lower and still make a profit. We believed them and stuck with them since we liked their product. Now we're *really* a good customer, one who stuck with them through an extremely depressed economy.

The question "Are you prepared to lose us as a customer today?" had tangible, real-world implications for the authors' business. The money we saved allowed us to avoid laying off a staff member. Some of the deepest satisfaction we get in running the business are times like these when our negotiation skills and hard work directly result in our company being able to keep its employees' families fed.

Lesson

For customers with solid track records, the question "Are you prepared to lose us as a customer today?" is a powerful motivator that usually results in excellent agreements. Lay the groundwork for this by getting competing quotes. For the question to be most effective, ask it in a polite, nonthreatening fashion.

How to Respond If You Are Asked "Are you prepared to lose us as a customer today?"

This is a tough question to answer if you do not have pricing flexibility. In this situation a measured response to this question could be "We very much value your business and would love to be able to serve you for many years to come. Unfortunately, you already have our best pricing. If you are on a limited budget we can certainly discuss providing a modified service or lower priced materials that could be within that budget." This response projects power but also floats an alternative of lower cost for less service.

If you do have flexibility in your pricing and are willing to meet any competing offer, this question is much easier to answer. In this scenario, your answer could be quite aggressive, "No. We will do whatever it takes to keep you satisfied. Give us any competing written quote and we will beat it."

Question #17

DO YOU REALIZE WE ARE THE SOLE SOURCE FOR THIS PRODUCT/SERVICE?

Any negotiator who is the sole source for a product or service is in the driver's seat when it comes to negotiations. When the person you are negotiating with comes to recognize you as the sole source of a product or service he will be faced with three choices:

1. *Not being able to obtain the product or service, which he may want or need.*

2. *Trying to find something else in the marketplace as good as your product or service as possible.*

3. *Agreeing to your terms and paying you what you want.*

The key prerequisite for successfully using this question is to position yourself so that your product or service is—or appears to be—unique. This work must be done in advance of the negotiation.

Once you have positioned yourself so that you appear to be the sole source of the product or service, a tactful way to get this point across is by simply asking the person you are negotiating with, "Do you realize we are the sole source for this product/service?" This question is a powerful one, with many repercussions for the recipient. These include:

- A shock for the recipient who was unaware of this fact

- The necessity to acknowledge the accuracy of the point

- An immediate loss of power in the negotiation by the recipient of the question

- A recognition that the proponent of the question
  - is aware of the fact that he is the sole source,
  - has all the power in the negotiation, and
  - is likely to use his position to extract whatever he wants to satisfy his needs

- A lowering of the expectations of the recipient

- Recognition that it may take an extraordinary offer to get this deal done

- Awareness that he may not be able to get a deal done with the person he's negotiating with

We have always sought to be in the position where the products and services that we sell are unique. Many of the products and services that we produce are unique and as such we are able to sell them at a hefty price. Where we have done so, we almost always make the person we are negotiating with aware of the fact that we are the sole source by politely asking, "Do you realize we are the sole source for this product/service?" Let's look at several examples of how we have used this question to phenomenal advantage.

In the early 1990s we came up with an idea for a new product. The American Medical Association sells approximately 50,000 copies per edition of a text called the *AMA Guides*. This text is required by law to be used by physicians when they examine people who have been injured at work and are filing claims for workers' compensation benefits. In a nutshell, the book shows physicians who examine workers how to determine how much money the injured workers are entitled to under the law.

The *AMA Guides* is very lengthy, complex, and difficult to use. Physicians struggle in understanding and using the book. We came up with the idea of creating instructional videotapes to explain to physicians how to use the *AMA Guides*. To produce the product, however, we needed the agreement and cooperation of the AMA.

After months of trying, we finally obtained an appointment with the AMA and flew out to their Chicago headquarters to meet them. The negotiation dialogue went something like this:

AUTHORS: As you know, we are proposing to do a series of instructional videos based on your *AMA Guides,* one video per chapter. We would explain how to use the book properly and sell the videos as a set for five times the price of the book. We would then split the revenue 50-50 between us and the AMA.

AMA (AFTER DISCUSSION AMONG THEMSELVES): Well, that is a great idea, no question about it. We can make a lot of money here, but we have one question. Why do we need you and your small company? We can just shoot the videos ourselves and keep 100 percent of the profit.

AUTHORS: Do you realize we are the sole source for these? We have signed the authors of the chapters of your book to exclusive contracts to do videos only for us. We have the talent locked up.
AMA (AFTER A SHOCKED LOOK AND SOME INTERNAL DISCUS-SION): Your proposal sounds great—50-50 it is. We will get legal to draw up a contract.

We made an almost immediate 400 percent return on invest-ment on the videos in the first four months alone. All told, we re-turned over 1500 percent on our original investment. The key to this eye-popping success was setting the stage by signing all the talent to exclusive deals so that we were the only persons who could produce the videos. Once this spadework was completed, it was relatively easy to ask the question "Do you realize we are the sole source for these?" and negotiate a very favorable deal.

In other parts of our business dealings, we constantly strive to produce something that either appears to be or is, in fact, unique. We are the only independent lawyers training expert witnesses in testifying skills. We created the only major conference on non-clinical careers for physicians (that is, for physicians who no longer want to work treating patients and would instead prefer other ca-reers, such as working for a pharmaceutical company or insurance company). We are the only lawyers providing one-on-one consult-ing for expert witnesses. The lesson is clear: If you want to be able to charge a premium, position yourself before the negotiation so that you are the sole source of a product or service and get this message across by asking, "Do you realize we are the sole source for these?" For example, we are frequently contacted by physicians who would like personal assistance in expanding their expert wit-ness practices. (Physicians commonly earn $500 to $1,000 per hour for serving as an expert witness in a legal dispute.) We are the only lawyers on the planet doing this. When a potential client questions our rates we remind them that we are the sole source, and this is always very helpful to our negotiating position.

Lesson

Positioning yourself to be the sole source and asking, "Do you realize we are the sole source for this product/service?" can lead to extraordinary negotiation results in which you are able to secure an extremely good price for your products or services.

How to Respond If You Are Asked "Do you realize we are the sole source for this product/service?"

There are two main ways to respond to this question. The first is to dispute the assertion that the other person is, in fact, a sole source. For example, "You're not the sole source—you never signed up the chapter coauthors and we can just use the coauthors to shoot the videos."

The second way to deal with this situation is most appropriate where the other party really is the sole source. In this scenario, you will want to respond in a way that will decrease the other party's power. The best way to do this is to stress how you don't really need what they are selling. For example, "That may very well be, but that doesn't change the fact that I don't really need what you have to offer because your exclusive contract covers only videos, and we could use the chapter authors to produce a CD-ROM or how-to book instead."

Question #18

WHAT ALTERNATIVES DO YOU HAVE?

This is a great question to use in almost any negotiation. The party who has the best alternatives usually has the most power in a negotiation since they don't need to deal—they have other options. The beauty of this question is that it forces the person you are negotiating with to express their alternatives. If the other person has no alternatives, you are placed in a very strong bargaining position. Even if he does express alternatives, this question helps move the negotiation forward and allows you to make points against these alternatives.

If you can determine that the other side really has no alternatives other than you, this is a very significant piece of information.

- **The fewer options or alternatives that the other side has, the more power you gain in the negotiation.**

- **The fact that the person you are negotiating with has not found alternatives (that you may know exist)**

tends to indicate that he is under severe time
pressure to get an agreement.

- You may be completely in the driver's seat and can
  completely control the negotiation and name your
  price.

When, in fact, you are able to determine that you are the only
show in town you become the sole source and many of the tradi-
tional rules of negotiating no longer apply.

The questions you should then ask yourself if you are in the
enviable position of being the sole source are:

- How badly does the other side need you?

- How much money is involved? That is, how much do
  they stand to lose if they cannot get you to agree?

- How hard are you willing to push them and risk
  their possibly walking away?

The thought process that the recipient of the question "What
alternatives do you have?" goes through is:

- I am reluctant to admit I have no alternatives.

- If I state falsely that I have alternatives and then am
  asked who/what they are, I will be unable to answer
  the question and my honesty and integrity will be
  called into question.

- If I anger the person I am negotiating with, he may
  ask an even more outrageous price to conclude the
  deal, or he may just walk away from it completely.

- I cannot afford to alienate my only potential source.

- I am better off just admitting my position and lack of alternatives and make the best of it.

Being able to ask "What alternatives do you have?" and get an honest answer can make huge differences in the results achieved in the negotiation. Let's look at some examples.

The owner of a health-service company we dealt with was moderately profitable. One day he received a call from a national company inquiring about the sale of his business. While he was eager to sell his company he wondered why a large national company would be interested in his small company. When he was unable to get a direct answer he asked the question "What alternatives do you have?" He was very pleasantly surprised to hear that they had no alternatives. He also learned the real reason for the sudden interest in his company. It turns out the national company wanted to open a branch immediately in his state and his company was the only one with the required licenses.

The owner of the company, after learning the real reason for the inquiry, was able to negotiate five times the average sale price of a company similar to his.

Here's an example from our own business. We were called by a prominent trial lawyer and asked to testify as an expert witness in a case. Here is how the discussion developed:

ATTORNEY: We would like to retain you to testify as an expert in a case, which involves the constitutionality of the Texas Workers' Compensation Act.

AUTHOR: I appreciate the offer, but I will have to decline because I have never testified as an expert and I am very busy with my law practice and other business interests.

ATTORNEY: We would really like to have you testify in this case due to the importance of the case.

AUTHOR: I am not trying to be difficult but why don't you get one of the other 10,000 workers' compensation lawyers to use as your expert?

ATTORNEY: Well, due to your stature in the field we would prefer you.

AUTHOR: What alternatives do you have?

ATTORNEY: Well, actually, you are the only attorney we have targeted because you are the only one who has written a book on the subject matter of this case.

AUTHOR: I am still very busy. How much money is involved?

ATTORNEY: Well, actually, there are billions of dollars riding on this lawsuit and I have been given a blank check to hire the best experts in the country and from around the world. We have hired twenty-two experts so far.

AUTHOR: What is the most you are paying any expert you have hired to date?

ATTORNEY: It is $500 an hour, but he is an internationally known expert.

AUTHOR: If you pay me $500 an hour from the time I leave my driveway in Falmouth, Massachusetts, until the time I return I will do it.

ATTORNEY: How much of retainer would you like?

AUTHOR: $10,000.

ATTORNEY: I will FedEx the check to you.

As an epilogue, asking the question "What alternatives do you have?" generated enough money from this one negotiation to pay for two years' tuition and room and board for Steve's daughter at a private college.

Here's one final example from our experiences to consider. Several years ago, we were expanding our business and were interested in hiring a recent business-school graduate. We were impressed by the graduate and made him a salary offer of what we could afford. He was greatly disappointed at the salary offer. Here's a verbatim transcript of the negotiation regarding salary. It took less than a minute and resulted in our paying not a dime over our original offer.

AUTHOR (EMPLOYER): The offer is $50,000 per year.
PROSPECTIVE EMPLOYEE (BIG FROWN): Well, that's really, really low. You realize I have an MBA? I can show you the statistics. The average business school graduate makes $90,000 on his first year out of school.
AUTHOR (EMPLOYER): If you have a competing offer for $90,000, I suggest you take it. What alternatives do you have?
PROSPECTIVE EMPLOYEE (4 to 5 seconds of silence): None.

The prospective employee called back the next day and accepted our offer. "What alternatives do you have?" reinforced his lack of bargaining power, allowed for a rapid and decisive negotiation, and made his choice of accepting the offer at hand an obvious one.

Before we finish, let's talk about the situation where the person you are negotiating with responds by stating their alternatives. This might be a bluff or it might be for real. Either way, you lose nothing by asking. When alternatives are presented, you can either probe further or you can counter these by letting them know what *your* alternatives are. Let's look at the last examples above and see how this might have played out had the prospective employee stated that they had alternatives.

AUTHOR (EMPLOYER): The offer is $50,000 per year.

PROSPECTIVE EMPLOYEE (BIG FROWN): Well, that's really, really low. You realize I have an MBA? I can show you the statistics. The average business school graduate makes $90,000 on his first year out of school.

AUTHOR (EMPLOYER): If you have a competing offer for $90,000, I suggest you take it. What alternatives do you have?

PROSPECTIVE EMPLOYEE (4 TO 5 SECONDS OF SILENCE): I am exploring many opportunities.

AUTHOR (EMPLOYER): Great. I wish you the best of luck. Our offer will remain open for twenty-four hours. We're going to make an offer to one of the other highly qualified persons we interviewed if we don't hear back from you before then. It was nice meeting you.

In this example, the employer was able to counter the vague alternatives suggested by the prospective employee by powerfully describing his own alternatives. Asking the question "What alternatives do you have?" served to move the negotiation forward rapidly and build negotiating power.

Lesson

"What alternatives do you have?" is a great question for almost any negotiating situation. You may find that the person you are negotiating with has no alternatives and that you are the sole source. If this happens you are in the driver's seat. Even if the person does state that they have alternatives, this question will move the negotiation forward, reveal important information, and provide a convenient opportunity for you to state your own alternatives—and thus build power in the negotiation.

How to Respond If You Are Asked "What alternatives do you have?"

There are different ways that you can respond to this question. The most obvious, as discussed above, is to offer a vague response such as "I have a good number of other irons in the fire" or the like. Such a response has the virtue of not explicitly admitting to the person that you don't have viable alternatives. The weakness, of course, is that by not getting into specifics, your alternatives may not seem credible.

The other way you can respond is to be prepared to clearly list your more attractive alternatives. For example, "I have a current pending employment offer for $80,000." Such an approach requires hard work and preparation. If you are able to truthfully give such a response you will have vastly increased your negotiating leverage.

Question #19

CAN I RECOMMEND SOMEONE ELSE?

The more power you have in a negotiation the better off you will be. One way to gain power is to give the person you are negotiating with the impression that you are highly in demand and not hungry for business. Asking "Can I recommend someone else?" is a simple and easy way to give just such an impression. The subtext of the question is direct and powerful: "I don't need your business. I am the best and unless you modify your positions, I am out of here." When asked during the right circumstances, "Can I recommend someone else?" can be extremely effective and will result in your gaining more favorable terms.

The best situation to use this question is where the parties are at an impasse and the person you are negotiating with has balked at your price or has provided you with a low offer that he will not improve on. Asking the question "Can I recommend someone else?" at this point ups the ante and challenges the power of the person you are negotiating with. This question is effective for many reasons, including:

- You are calling the bluff of the person you are negotiating with and indicating quite clearly that you are ready, willing, and able to walk away from the bargaining table.

- The person you are negotiating with has to reassess his expectation and positions if he wants to get the deal done with you.

- You are exuding supreme confidence as not only are you apparently willing to walk away but you are also willing to recommend another provider, presumably a competitor.

This question is best used after you have developed a reputation for being a high-quality provider of whatever services you provide. Key to the effectiveness of "Can I recommend someone else?" is the person you are negotiating with believing that the services you offer are in some way uniquely valuable. To position yourself to use this question you must work hard at finding a niche and building a reputation for superior or unique value.

Be aware that "Can I recommend someone else?" is a question that is somewhat risky. In many circumstances, the person you are negotiating with might very well take you up on your offer. As such, using this question as a bluff when you have been offered a price that you consider acceptable but not ideal or where the person you are negotiating with is shopping around can be counterproductive and result in losing an opportunity for business.

As discussed above, the best time you can use this question is when you have predetermined that the person you are negotiating with has already bought into your reputation and value. A good way to find this out is to determine during your preliminary negotiations how the person found out about you.* If they found out about you through recommendations and reputation, "Can I recommend someone else?" can be a great question to use if needed. If, on the other hand, the person you are negotiating with is calling everyone in the phone book, this question is likely to be counterproductive since the person has not bought into your reputation, is shopping around, and may be more concerned with price than quality.

You always run the risk that the person you are negotiating with will say okay, whom do you recommend? Because of this, you need to be prepared to give one or two recommendations. Giving such recommendations should usually not be considered a failure. If the terms offered to you don't make sense to you, walking away from the deal is usually much better than having a deal that makes no economic sense. Also, if the person you are negotiating with appears to be a troublemaker or difficult to deal with, referring the business out could very much be in your best interest.

One final advantage of "Can I recommend someone else?" is that it can ingratiate yourself with one of your competitors. Referring business that does not make economic sense to you to a competitor can be a shrewd course of action. This is because your competitor will usually return the favor in the future if they have potential business that doesn't fit their model, that they are too busy to take, or that they can't accept, say because of a conflict of interest.

Oftentimes the person you sent to the competitor will not tell the competitor how they got the competitor's name. If you do recommend someone else it's a best practice to give your own heads-up to the person you recommended. This can be done with a quick phone call or e-mail.

We use "Can I recommend someone else?" all the time during our negotiations when clients are looking to hire us for training or consulting. One of the reasons we are able to do so is that we have

* See Question #1.

worked hard to develop a superb reputation in a narrow niche that has few competitors. Here's how the negotiation typically goes. Note how we verify in advance of using "Can I recommend someone else?" what the potential client believes about our reputation.

ORGANIZATION: We would like to have you come in and do a two-day training session for our group. What kind of rate can you offer us?

AUTHORS: How did you find out about us?

ORGANIZATION: The board has had three recommendations from members who have seen you in action and were extremely impressed.

AUTHORS: A few questions: where and when is it; what is the topic; how many people are expected to attend; and what are you charging them to attend?

ORGANIZATION: It is in Napa, California, April 15th; the topic is Testifying Skills; we hope to get 150 people to attend; and we will charge $200 per person.

AUTHORS: We can do it for the all-inclusive price of $15,000. That includes our travel expenses and detailed handbooks for each attendee.

ORGANIZATION: That is way over our budget. We had planned on spending less than $2,500.

AUTHORS: I see. Can I recommend someone else? A local attorney perhaps might fit your needs. I have someone in the Bay Area in mind.

ORGANIZATION: Do you know how lovely it is in Napa in the springtime? The hotel has a wonderful spa that your spouses would love. You'd be getting tremendous exposure, too. Many of our members are movers and shakers.

AUTHORS: Well, that sounds enticing, but the way we do the training is a huge commitment of time on our end. We prepare and study. Also, the travel from and back to the East Coast will eat up two full days. If you want, I could ask around for you for someone who might be willing to throw something together within your budget? In any event, it has been a pleasure—

ORGANIZATION: Wait! Let's not get hasty here. Let me get back to you.... *(Two hours later.)* Good news! We will raise the registration fee to $300—so we can afford your $15,000 fee.

Of course, sometimes the person we are negotiating with takes us up on our offer to recommend someone else. Here's how those negotiations typically go.

POTENTIAL CLIENT: I have been to a few of your seminars and would like to explore hiring you as a consultant. What is the fee?

AUTHORS: We charge $500 an hour or a flat fee depending on the assignment.

POTENTIAL CLIENT: That is quite expensive. My budget is only $1,500.

AUTHORS: Can I recommend someone else?

POTENTIAL CLIENT: That would be great.

AUTHORS: Try Mickey Donovan at 555-555-1234. He is much cheaper than us.

POTENTIAL CLIENT: Thanks!

Even though we lost the deal, asking "Can I recommend someone else?" in this situation was the right thing to do. First, the question offered us a chance to improve our bargaining position. There was every chance that he would have just agreed to our terms after we asked the question. That didn't work out in this case, but what did happen was that we were able to quickly determine that this was a client looking for $7,500 worth of services for $1,500. Such a gap is not likely to be closed through negotiating. As such, this is a client that it is better to walk away from as soon as possible. We were able to walk away while leaving a positive impression in the client's mind. In addition, since we followed up by shooting our competitor Mickey Donovan an e-mail about the recommendation, we have built goodwill with him. All in all, asking "Can I recommend someone else?" was a no-lose proposition for us.

Lesson

"Can I recommend someone else?" is a question that can greatly improve your bargaining position in that you appear ready to walk away from the negotiation. This question is not without risk. The risk is that you will be taken up on your offer and your prospect will walk away. "Can I recommend someone else?" is therefore best used when you are far apart on terms (and hence have little to lose), where you have a superior reputation (so that price comparisons with your competitors is an apples-to-oranges exercise), and where it is fairly clear that your reputation matters to the person you are negotiating with such that they are not simply looking for the lowest possible price.

How to Respond If You Are Asked "Can I recommend someone else?"

The answer to this question should be "I'd love to work something out with you, but I would appreciate any referrals you can make." This answer avoids a "no," which would eviscerate your bargaining position. It's also somewhat less than an unqualified "yes" and as such, allows you to keep negotiating with the person who asked the question.

Question #20

HOW MUCH BUSINESS DO YOU THINK WE CAN DO IN THE FUTURE IF WE CAN WRAP UP THIS NEGOTIATION SUCCESSFULLY?

When there appears to be a realistic opportunity for substantial, recurring future business between the parties, the entire dynamic of the negotiation can and often does change. This question is designed to bring to the forefront the potential for future business that the person you are negotiating with has at stake. This realization will markedly increase your negotiating leverage.

Customers who can turn into repeat business are hugely more valuable than one-shot deals. A deal that is worth $10,000 profit for the person you are negotiating with can be thought of as worth $100,000 over ten years if the relationship turns into a long-term, annual one.

By asking this question, you are strongly hinting at the possibility of becoming a long-term client. When you ask "How much business do you think we can do in the future if we can wrap up this negotiation successfully?" the person you are negotiating with will probably:

- Start to run the numbers in his head. For example: 3 deals per year x 5 years x $150,000 per deal = $2,250,000. This clearly raises the stakes of the negotiation. Instead of potentially losing a $150,000 deal, he is now faced with losing $2,250,000.

- Begin to consider leaving more on the table to get his foot in the door to obtain Deal #1.

- Start to develop the "story" he will tell superiors explaining why he made so many concessions when negotiating Deal #1.

- Consider doing Deal #1 as a loss leader. It could be worth it to secure a new long-term customer.

The subtext of the question is pretty clear and intended to be so: If we cannot reach an agreement there will be no additional deals and all my potential future business will be lost. The beauty of this question is that it can be used in many different types of negotiations and doesn't have any real downside. The person you are negotiating with may try to lock in your commitment for future deals, but this can be easily parried by politely saying, "Let's worry about the future later. I want to see how well you perform on this order."

Dangling the possibility of future orders in front of the person you are negotiating with is a simple and easy way of increasing your negotiating power and getting better deals. We use this technique in many of our negotiations. For example, when negotiating with a freelance Web page designer a few years ago, we conducted a negotiation that went something like this:

AUTHORS: We would like you to design a simple Web site for one of our expert witness clients to help them promote themselves to the attorneys who might want to hire them.

DESIGNER: I would be happy to work with you. A simple Web site with no real bells and whistles is $5,000.

AUTHORS: That is out of our price range.

DESIGNER: I do not even like to take on these small jobs as they eat up a lot of time and the clients can be quite demanding . . . $4,000 is probably the—

AUTHORS: I feel you should know that we have 1,300 expert witness clients and many of them need Web pages. Once we find someone we can work with who does a high-quality job we will be recommending that firm to our 1,300 experts. How much business do you think we can handle in the future if we can wrap up this negotiation successfully? You're a solo freelancer—how much new business do you think you could successfully handle?

DESIGNER: Yes, I can do it. I can do this one for $3,000 bottom line. How soon will you be making a decision about directing your other 1,300 clients here?

By suggesting the possibility of future work in front of the Web designer (but in no way committing to future work), we were able to get his price down a full 40 percent. This was the direct result of asking a simple, enticing, nonoffensive, and nonconfrontational question.

Here's another example. A few years ago, we were looking to change our mail-house vendor. The mail house is the entity that does our bulk mailings. We set up a face-to-face meeting. At the meeting we asked, "How much business do you think we can do in the future if we can wrap up this negotiation successfully?" We could see the mail-house owner's eyes light up as soon as we asked this. The end result was a very competitive price that was a win-win since we did, in fact, end up sending the mail house more than a million pieces of mail each year for the last seven-plus years.

Lesson

"How much business do you think we can do in the future if we can wrap up this negotiation successfully?" is a powerful, almost risk-free question because the potential for future business can be a nearly irresistible lure to many of the hungry businesspeople you will be negotiating with.

How to Respond If You Are Asked "How much business do you think we can do in the future if we can wrap up this negotiation successfully?"

The best way to respond to this question is to try to get a firm agreement to make the deal long-term. For example, "If you agree to sign up for three years we can take 5 percent off." If you are able to successfully lock in multiple years' worth of business you will have likely made a great coup. Unfortunately, a sophisticated negotiator probably won't agree to get locked in long-term. This response is certainly worth a try, however.

Another way to respond to this question is in such a way that shows that although you are certainly interested in repeat business you are not going off the deep end in excitement. Such a response could be, "Well, we love repeat profitable business, but each deal we make has to be worth the time and effort we put into it. Let's find a win-win solution here and then, hopefully, we can do business together for many years to come." The idea here is to encourage a long-term relationship but indicate that you are not overeager and that you need to be fairly compensated.

Question #21

ARE YOU AWARE THAT [SOME FACT THAT SUGGESTS THAT MONEY IS TIGHT]?

It's one thing to suggest to someone during a negotiation that you won't do something. It is often a lot easier to show that you *can't* do something. Crying poor-mouth can be a very effective negotiating technique. Asking any one of the following variations such as: "Are you aware we simply do not have that kind of money?" is an easy and effective way to make the point that you simply can't afford the offered terms and get a better deal when negotiating to buy something.

"Are you aware that our budget is limited?" is best used when you are the buyer and are trying to negotiate a lower price. The subtexts of the question are simple, namely: Money is a concern. Price is a big issue, and even if I wanted to pay the price you are offering, I probably can't. I just can't afford it.

The question itself is low risk. The one time this question is very risky and should not be used is the situation where you are asking the seller to lend you money as part of the deal. Crying poor-mouth in that circumstance can be counterproductive since you will be making yourself appear to be less creditworthy.

"Are you aware that [some fact that suggests that money is tight]?" has many advantages. First, the question puts the focus on your ability to pay, not the product in question. This can make the negotiation less contentious since you are not challenging or criticizing the product or service of the person you are negotiating with.

Another big advantage is the question gives you wiggle room. Here's what we mean. By asking "Are you aware that we are having a tough year?" you are strongly implying, but do not outright say, that money is tight and you need a great deal. Asking this question does not, however, back you into a corner that could end the negotiation in failure, for example by saying, "Money is very tight here, we can't pay a dime over $1,000." In this circumstance you would have backed yourself into a corner by crying poor-mouth in a particularly inflexible manner.

A final advantage is that, when asked properly, this question can make the person you are negotiating with feel empathy toward you. The person you are negotiating with is a human being. It's natural for them to want to give the best deals to people they like and that they have empathy for.

Consider as well the likely thought process of the person you are negotiating with. When faced with "Are you aware that my husband just lost his job?" that person is likely to conclude that since you can't get blood from a stone he had better give you a good price. If he gets greedy and asks for too much he's probably going to lose the deal and end up with nothing because you are either very cost conscious or simply don't have the money to pay a premium price.

"Are you aware that the stock market just lost over 40 percent of its value?" is best deployed either at the very beginning of a negotiation or when there begins to be a breakdown over price. Using this question preemptively at the beginning of the negotiation can be quite effective in reducing the expectations of the person you are negotiating with. Using this question when a dispute on price comes up can break a potential deadlock and move the price to your own advantage.

We have used variations of this question many, many times to our advantage in both our personal and business lives.

In the fall of 2008, we were negotiating to hire a computer programmer to do some IT work for us. We received a quote of $35,000 for the work. We could afford to pay only $10,000 for the work in question. The quote was so far beyond what we had budgeted that we decided not to try to haggle on price, but rather just to find someone else in our price range. We gave the programmer a courtesy call and weren't even trying to negotiate with him. Here's about how the call went:

> **AUTHOR:** Thanks for the quote. Now that I am breathing again I figured I'd give you a call. I'm sure you are superb, but this is well beyond our price range. We'll have to find someone less expensive.
> **PROGRAMMER:** You guys have been in business for thirty years and are both lawyers, and you can't afford me?
> **AUTHOR:** Are you aware that our business is off 50 percent because of the recession? Our main business lines are training and consulting. Most corporations have strictly banned travel, continuing education, and consulting. It's a real triple hit we've taken.
> **PROGRAMMER:** I'm sorry, I wasn't aware of that. I wish you the best of luck.

A week later, the programmer called back and agreed to a scaled-down version of the job for our $10,000 budget. We were able to come to an agreement partly through a mutual scale-down of the specs of the job to its essential elements and partly because of the programmer's realization that we just could not afford to pay the price he had originally offered. "Are you aware that our business is off 50 percent because of the recession?" instantly changed the tone and course of the negotiations.

This technique is so effective that it can even be used with utilities and other companies you thought you couldn't negotiate with. We used this question successfully with the phone company for one of the author's home phone recently:

> **AUTHOR:** Hi, I am one of your customers and wanted to see if you have any better rates? I'm thinking about giving up the landline phone all together and just using the cell phone.
>
> **PHONE COMPANY:** Sir, you should be very careful before doing that. You'll have a lot of dropped calls and you might not have a phone if the battery is dead and you need one in an emergency.
>
> **AUTHOR:** Yes, I would love to keep your service, but it's the cost that's the problem. Are you aware that my wife's in the banking industry? She's our breadwinner. They are laying off tens of thousands of people a week. We are very, very concerned that she's going to lose her job, and we need to save as much money as possible.
>
> **PHONE COMPANY:** Let me see if there are any specials or promotions that could help you.... Oh, here's one, how about $20 off your bill each month for the next year?
>
> **AUTHOR:** That would work for us. Let's do it.

We've also used this technique with our landlord. For the past thirty years, each and every year our rent has gone up. Recently, we asked for a lease extension. We sent an e-mail to our landlord that was something like this:

> *Dear Bob:*
> *Are you aware that our business is off over 50 percent*
> *because of the recession? We are exploring our options in*
> *terms of our lease and are looking to save money. How much*
> *of a rent reduction can you provide for us for a new lease?*

We received a lease back with a rent reduction in Year 1 and flat rents for Years 2 and 3. The message of the question was very powerful. We just can't afford rent increases. The money isn't there. The preemptive use of the question "Are you aware that our business is off over 50 percent because of the recession?" set the tone of the negotiation and helped forestall rent increases and better yet, get us a rent reduction.

Lesson

Crying poor-mouth can be an effective way to communicate that you simply can't afford to pay the premium price that has been demanded. Asking, "Are you aware that [some fact that suggests that money is tight]?" can be a very effective and low-risk way to help obtain a favorable price when buying a product or service. This question can be used equally effectively in business or personal negotiations since the person you are negotiating with will be left to ponder whether he is risking the deal by not being more flexible on his price.

How to Respond If You Are Asked "Are you aware that (some fact that suggests that money is tight)?"

A good way to respond to this question is in such a way that makes the point that what you are offering will save or make the other party money. For example, "I'm sorry to hear that, but the good news is that this is all the more reason you'll want to take our course that will show you how to make $500 per hour as an expert witness."

Another way to respond to a question like this is to turn things around and stress how your costs have gone up. The message here is clear: Although I'd like to help you, I just can't—my cost structure won't allow it. For example, "Yeah, I hear you and feel your pain. With the health insurance increases and tax increases we've faced our costs are way up this year, too. I truly wish I had more room to help you out."

Question #22

DO YOU REALIZE THAT YOUR COMPETITOR IS CHARGING A LOWER PRICE?

One of the strongest pieces of leverage a buyer has is the ability and willingness to buy from a competitor of the seller you are negotiating with. If this happens, the seller will lose the deal. Asking "Do you realize that your competitor is charging a lower price?" is an easy, polite, low-risk, and powerfully credible way to implicitly threaten to go to a competitor and thus get the lowest price possible from a seller.

The subtexts of "Do you realize that your competitor is charging a lower price?" are clear and powerful. Namely: I have done my homework. I have found a better price from one of your competitors. If you don't beat—or at least meet—the competitor's price, I'm going to buy from the competitor and you're out of luck.

Here's what we suggest in terms of how and when to most effectively deploy "Do you realize that your competitor is charging a lower price?" You should first shop around and do your homework. Get as many prices as is reasonable, or a minimum of three. Then decide which vendor (price aside) you would prefer to do business with, say, because you like their service or they are conveniently located. Go to that vendor and negotiate a price. If you reach a favorable price that is lower than the competition, push the vendor as hard as you can and then take the deal. If, however, you reach a sticking point higher than a competitor's price ask, "Do you realize that your competitor is charging a lower price?"

Asking "Do you realize that your competitor is charging a lower price?" is low risk as long as you do not ask this too early in the negotiation (we'll discuss this further below). The worst the seller is likely to say is that he can't come down on his price. This is usually done by the seller somehow trying to say that you are comparing apples to oranges in that his product, service, or brand is somewhat different than his competitor's. If the seller tries this apples-to-oranges defense on you, feel free to push back by again focusing on your alternatives. The implicit and credible threat of going to a competitor will usually be extremely effective. For example:

> **BUYER:** Do you realize that your competitor is charging a lower price?
> **SELLER:** Well, we have a different level of service. We've been in this business for thirty years and they are a start-up.
> **BUYER:** So you won't beat their price?
> **SELLER:** I didn't say that—of course, we will. We have better service and low prices. That's our value proposition.

"Do you realize that your competitor is charging a lower price?" is a very good question to ask since it puts the person you are negotiating with in a very difficult situation. A seller who is asked this question will refuse to reduce his price to meet the competition only at the acute risk of losing the deal. If the seller can come down and meet or beat the competitor's price, he usually will. If the seller can't or won't come down, you maintain the option of going with the low price you have in hand from the competition. We use this bedrock negotiation technique and question constantly and to great effect. Some examples:

A few years ago, one of the authors was assisting his elderly uncle to buy a new car. We looked around and my uncle picked out the model and trim he liked. I called around to about six or seven dealers within fifty miles of my uncle's house and got prices. This took about an hour. Armed with numerous competing quotes we walked into the car dealer down the street from my uncle's house where, for convenience purposes, he'd strongly prefer to buy the car. Here's about how the negotiation went:

> **AUTHOR:** What's your asking price?
> **SALESMAN:** We can offer you the car at $22,500.
> **AUTHOR:** Wow. More than I was expecting. Can you take $21,800?
> **SALESMAN:** I'll tell you what. I can come down to $22,400.
> **AUTHOR:** Are you aware that we have a quote from a nearby dealer for $21,999?
> **SALESMAN:** We'll beat that. Thanks for the heads-up. We can do $21,998.
> **AUTHOR:** Done.

Note how we had waited until *after* the dealer had quoted us a price and we had tried to negotiate him down before mentioning competing offers. The reason for this is simple. You don't want to tip your hand too soon. What if the dealer's ask price came in lower than our competing bids, say at $21,899? If the ask price does come in lower than your competing bids you can try to negotiate, but you certainly should not mention that all the other bids you received were higher. For example:

AUTHOR: What's your asking price?

SALESMAN: We can offer you the car at $21,899.

AUTHOR: How much flexibility do you have in your price?

SALESMAN: Not much.

AUTHOR: If you can do $21,699, you've got a deal.

SALESMAN: The best we can do is $21,799.

AUTHOR: Done.

By not tipping our hand we were able to negotiate a price $200 lower than the low bid we had received from the competitors. Once you reveal your best alternate price you will never get a much better price. As such, you should never reveal the competitor's prices until after you have reached a deadlock on price.

One more quick example about not tipping your hand too early. One of the authors recently quoted out putting a brick walkway from his front door to his driveway. Vendor #1 quoted out $9,000. We called Vendor #2. When talking to Vendor #2, we never mentioned the price from Vendor #1. Vendor $2 quoted a price of $4,200. Had we prematurely asked Vendor #2 if he were aware that Vendor #1 was charging $9,000, Vendor #2 would likely have come in much higher than $4,200 since he then knew what our alternatives were.

We use this fundamental technique all the time in our business and personal lives. We recently negotiated a six-figure printing contract. By getting a competing bid and confronting our preferred vendor with it we were able to save more than $25,000. Getting the competing bids took about two to three hours. That works out to around $10,000 a hour, which is a pretty satisfying rate of return on your time.

One final story. Very recently, during the time we were writing this book, one of the authors was talking to some relatives, who explained how a pipe had burst in their house and how they had to do all types of repairs. One thing that needed to be done is that they needed to replace a heat pump.

"Wow, how much is one of those?" the author asked.

"Well, they quoted us $8,000, but I got them down to $4,000," replied the relative.

"You know, I'm writing a book on negotiating. Can I ask how did you do it?"

"I got a competing quote for $4,250, and told the guy that he was way high. He came right down and beat his competitor's price."

The relative was able to negotiate a 50 percent price reduction by diligently shopping around and getting competing prices. Time spent researching and shopping around on major purchases is almost always well spent. Do your homework and you will be able to negotiate very favorable prices by playing one seller off against another.

Lesson

Confronting a seller with a lower price from one of the seller's competitors by asking "Do you realize that your competitor is charging a lower price?" can be dramatically effective in quickly and easily obtaining often large price reductions. This technique is low risk as long as you do not tip your hand too early. The key to effective use of this question is doing your homework first. Only once your homework of getting competing bids is completed should you negotiate with the seller you prefer to do business with.

How to Respond If You Are Asked "Do you realize that your competitor is charging a lower price?"

As mentioned above, the best way to respond to this question is to try to credibly differentiate the product or service that is offered by the competition. In effect, your argument is that they are comparing apples to oranges. For example, "What they quoted you was a four-cylinder without a moonroof. That's why they are so low. What you asked me for is the six-cylinder with the moonroof."

Another good way to respond to this question is to appear very skeptical. One way to do this is to ask if the other party got the quote in writing since you'd like to see the details. If you are provided with the details, study them carefully and try to come up with arguments as to why what you are selling is more valuable and different. Another way to get across the skeptical message is to bombard the other party with questions that imply skepticism about the competing quote and might make them nervous about what they could get themselves into with the competition. For example, "I assume the permitting and engineering is not included in that? They also can't be using two-by-six construction?" or "Yes, the home heating oil is twenty cents per gallon cheaper, but the supplier will not come out when your furnace stops working at 2 A.M."

In the situation where your competitor really does have a lower price for the same service, your best response is probably to graciously acknowledge this fact and try to close the deal. For example, "I appreciate your pointing that out. We always offer the lowest prices and would be more than pleased to beat that for you." This approach, of course, assumes that you can beat the price and still make a profit.

PART VI

A Much Bigger Pie

INTRODUCTION: The most satisfying negotiations are often those that result in win-win results. Win-win negotiations can result in mutually beneficial long-term relationships. Indeed, in many circumstances you are much better off if the other party is also satisfied with the results of the negotiation. The reason for this is simply that if the other party is not happy, they won't want to do business with you in the future and you will need to spend valuable time and money finding someone else. The questions in this section are designed to help you leverage the possibility and/or promise of a win-win negotiating result.

Question #23

INSTEAD OF FIGHTING ABOUT HOW TO DIVIDE
UP THIS RELATIVELY SMALL PIE, WILL YOU
AGREE TO TRY TO FIND A WAY TO MAKE
A MUCH BIGGER PIE THAT WE CAN SHARE?

Success in life and business is often built upon forming and nurtur-
ing mutually profitable long-term relationships. "Instead of fighting
about how to divide up this relatively small pie, will you agree to
try to find a way to make a much bigger pie that we can share?" is a
question designed to facilitate the formation of mutually beneficial
long-term relationships. The subtext of the question is simply that
if we can just agree to work together instead of against each other,
we will both likely be better off.

Under most circumstances, the authors are strong believers in
win-win negotiations. In such negotiations, both parties are satisfied with the results. The reason for this is simple. If the person we
are doing business with is making a profit and happy, that person
will want to do business with us again in the future. If they are not
happy, we will sooner or later need to find a new partner. The new

partner might not be as good as the old one and we will expend time and money finding and negotiating with a replacement. "Instead of fighting about how to divide up this relatively small pie, will you agree to try to find a way to make a much bigger pie that we can share?" is a great question to ask if you'd like to try to turn a win-lose negotiation into a win-win negotiation.

"Instead of fighting about how to divide up this relatively small pie, will you agree to try to find a way to make a much bigger pie that we can share?" is an effective question to ask partly because of its wording. That wording makes it almost irresistible. Who could say "no" to wanting to make a bigger pie or at least find out how to do so? How can one resist the premise that the deal needs to work for both parties to the negotiation?

In fact, the response to the question "How can we build a bigger pie here" is almost always positive. You can expect one of the following typical responses:

- **Sure—what do you have in mind?**

- **Sounds good—how do we start?**

- **Should we start small and build upon our success?**

- **What kinds of things would help you here?**

- **What I really need is x and y.**

- **Would changing payment terms, scope of the agreement, delivery date, or increasing or decreasing the quality help us here?**

Once the person you are negotiating with responds in the affirmative to this question, it will be much easier to find a win-win solution. There are many reasons for this, including:

- The negotiation is no longer assumed to be a zero-sum game with one winner and one loser.

- The parties, when working together, will usually exchange information more freely.

- The parties can speak more frankly about their needs, goals, interests, and desires.

- There is a recognition that both parties are interested in forming a long-term, mutually profitable relationship.

- To make the relationship work, the parties are sincerely interested in making sure that the person they are negotiating with does, in fact, succeed.

- Assuring the success of the party you are negotiating with gives incentives for them to live up to the agreement.

- The I-win-you-lose tension of the negotiation is diffused.

- The parties start to look jointly for creative solutions.

- Trust is created between the parties.

- The chances of a deadlock are substantially reduced.

- Emphasis is placed on creating new business opportunities, synergy, and the possibility of future agreements.

- A cooperative problem-solving approach is less contentious, less stressful, and more enjoyable for many negotiators.

- The relationship between the parties is recognized as being more important than the conflict.

"Instead of fighting about how to divide up this relatively small pie, will you agree to try to find a way to make a much bigger pie that we can share?" is best asked when negotiations have stalled but prior to the point that the parties are entrenched in their respective positions. It's a real feel-good question that can rapidly evaporate tension and can help the formation of mutually beneficial long-term relationships. We have used this question countless times in our own negotiations to great success.

For example, back in the 1990s, we were looking to expand our business's presence on the Internet. We wanted to create an online store for ordering and a home page that was content rich, frequently updated, search engine optimized, properly maintained, and generated large amounts of 24/7 sales. We didn't have the in-house manpower to do this so we decided to hire someone.

We settled on a very intelligent recent graduate from a top law school (we'll call him Sandy). Sandy was the type of person who can be hard to find away from a big city. We started negotiating with Sandy. The problem was that if Sandy worked in a big law firm as he was qualified to do, he would command a six-figure salary. On one hand, we could not afford to pay Sandy a six-figure salary. On the other hand, we recognized that even if we got Sandy for short money (i.e., we win, he loses), he might be very likely to leave when the first better offer came along.

After going back and forth on salary for a period of time we tried a different approach. We asked Sandy, "This obviously needs to work for both of us so instead of fighting about how to divide up this relatively small pie, will you agree to try to find a way to make a much bigger pie that we can share?" He readily agreed. We explained how we understood his value, talents, academic pedigree, and potential. We also explained how we weren't a big-city law firm sitting on tons of cash. We then were able to work together to quickly agree to a compensation formula whereby Charlie would receive a decent salary, which we could afford, along with a guaranteed bonus of a percentage of gross sales generated from our e-commerce sites.

The agreement was a true win-win and there were good feelings on all sides. We were more than happy to share the bigger pie with Sandy if he could make one for us with e-commerce sales. In the meantime, we weren't committed to a guaranteed salary we could not afford. Sandy recognized that with this deal his earning potential was actually *higher* than what he would make at a law firm. We all understood that Sandy would be motivated to boost sales. Sandy worked for us for many years and quickly grew our e-commerce revenues from nothing into the significant percentage of our business that they represent today.

Lesson

Turning a competitive zero-sum (I win, you lose) negotiation into a win-win search for mutual success can be achieved by asking "Instead of fighting about how to divide up this relatively small pie, will you agree to try to find a way to make a much bigger pie that we can share?" The question is very hard to resist. It almost always results in a positive response from the person you are negotiating with. Once the person you are negotiating with buys into the concept of creating a bigger pie, it will be much easier to reach a win-win deal that will be profitable to both parties to the negotiation.

How to Respond If You Are Asked
"Instead of fighting about how to divide up this relatively small pie, will you agree to try to find a way to make a much bigger pie that we can share?"

This is not an adversarial or trick question. The best way to answer it is a simple "Absolutely, what do you have in mind?" This response will hopefully result in a creative win-win proposal that you can then carefully consider.

Question #24

HOW ABOUT WE TRY IT FOR A WHILE; WHAT DO WE HAVE TO LOSE?

Not all negotiations involve adversaries. Indeed, some of the most personally and financially consequential negotiations you will ever be involved with involve colleagues, business associates, and family members. "How about we try it for a while; what do we have to lose?" is a superb question to ask in many negotiations.

The subtexts of "How about we try it for a while; what do we have to lose?" are very powerful, namely: We are on the same team. I only am proposing something that I think will work out for both of us. If it doesn't work out, we don't have to continue. There is little to be lost by not trying it out.

"How about we try it for a while; what do we have to lose?" is remarkably effective. The reason it is so effective is that it is almost impossible to resist. The person you are negotiating with will be very hard pressed to answer "no" to this question. There are many reasons for this, including:

- Since there is nothing to lose, what is the harm in trying this?

- What could be more reasonable than to try it out it and see what happens?

- The person requesting this is a family member, associate, or colleague. To say "no" to such a reasonable proposal could damage this relationship.

- You are implicitly agreeing in your question that if it doesn't work, you will withdraw your request.

If you want to make this question work, it is critical to form a proposal that can be tried at little risk. There are usually two aspects to this. First, what you are proposing needs to be able to be easily undone. Second, there should be no risk of high cost, reputation damage, or other irreparable harm from your proposal.

You should also be flexible in your proposal. Many times, the person you are asking "How about we try it for a while; what do we have to lose?" may have legitimate questions on concerns regarding the risk involved, the terms of the trial arrangement, the length of the trial arrangement, or how success or failure is measured. You need to be prepared to modify your proposal to meet such legitimate concerns.

If the person you ask "How about we try it for a while; what do we have to lose?" responds in the negative, you will likely want to ask why. The answer will usually be that there is too much risk involved in trying out the proposal. If that is the case, you need to be prepared to articulate why you feel there is little risk in seeing what happens. Flexibility in your proposal so that the risk is reduced can also be quite helpful.

"How about we try it for a while; what do we have to lose?" is one of the most effective negotiating questions we use in our intracompany negotiations. Our business is run by four partners. We are a diverse group with different backgrounds and experiences. Two things each of the four of us has in common, however, is that we are each very strong willed and are very confident in our own ideas.

Running a business, especially one in a niche field, is an art and not a science. There is no book to look up what to do. Also, in many cases, there is not past precedent you can easily turn to that will tell you exactly what to do in a situation. These factors make running a business challenging, but also intellectually stimulating.

When faced with an internal decision in our business about what to do where there is not precedent, the single most powerful and successful negotiating question that can be used is "How about we try it for a while; what do we have to lose?" One such area is new product development. When deciding whether to develop a new product, we have to balance the potential risk against the potential reward. Case in point was a recent service the authors' company developed for physicians. One of the authors was advocating a service where physicians would pay our company a yearly fee and we would promote the physicians to insurance companies to try to get the physicians consulting assignments involving the review of medical files. Here's how the negotiations went:

AUTHOR: I have a great idea. I think we should develop a National Directory of Medical File Review Consultants. I ran the numbers. We charge our doctors $395 a year and publish their info online and in a print directory, which we promote to insurance companies. We could make a lot of money and it's a sustainable product.

RESISTANT PARTNERS: Your last idea cost us $50,000. We're still recovering from that one.

AUTHOR: This time is different. I have conducted a detailed survey of our customer/clients and they have shown high enthusiasm for the idea of a National Directory of Medical File Review Consultants.

RESISTANT PARTNERS: We don't buy it. We've used needs assessments in the past that have shown interest, then, when push comes to shove, the product doesn't sell. Besides, the doctors won't want this work since it only pays $100 to $200 a hour.

AUTHOR: I put that number in the needs assessment. They still say they want it.

RESISTANT PARTNERS: Well, what if you can't get the doctors consulting work? That will damage our reputation and brand.

AUTHOR: Already thought of that. We'll give the docs a full money-back guarantee for nine months. If they aren't happy we give them their money back. What do they have to lose?

RESISTANT PARTNERS: We still don't think this will work. That's what our intuition says.

AUTHOR: How about we try it out; what do we have to lose? I can send out an initial test-marketing piece. If not enough doctors sign up we'll refund their money and forget about the whole thing without spending the development money to actually create the directory's infrastructure. If, on the other hand, we get the good response I am expecting, we can invest in creating the infrastructure. In that case, we'll have a sustainable product that can generate money indefinitely.

RESISTANT PARTNERS: Assuming you don't spend more than $20,000 on the start-up and initial marketing costs, we can live with this.

AUTHOR: Agreed. If the result is poor I'll be the first one to recommend pulling the plug on this. We'll risk $20,000 versus the chance to make a $50,000 to $100,000 annual profit indefinitely. Let's give it a fair chance, though, and see what happens.

The author was able to prevail in this negotiation because he developed a business plan that was low risk (delaying many development costs until after the product was actually sold) and high potential reward (annual, sustainable product). It was also easy to get out from under if things didn't work out (we would just refund the money of the orders we had received and fold it up). Under these circumstances, it was almost impossible for his partners to refuse the suggestion of just trying it out. It's a good thing the author used the question, too, because the test mailing ended up generating a very good response. Without "How about we try it out; what do we have to lose?" this valuable new product never would have gotten off the ground.

Here's another example of "How about we try it out; what do we have to lose?" It involved one of the most satisfying, successful, and rewarding negotiations ever conducted by Nancy, the wife of one of the authors. Some background here. At the time when Nancy had her first child a few years ago, she worked at a big bank. She wanted to spend more time with her newborn. Her company had a policy whereby employees could work flexible schedules "at the approval and in the discretion of their supervisors." She asked her boss if she could take Fridays off and work longer days Monday through Thursday to make up the time. Her boss was very hesitant. Here's about how the negotiation went:

> **NANCY:** Now that I'm back from maternity leave, I'd like to explore with you the possibility of staying home Fridays with the baby, and working longer hours Monday through Thursday.
>
> **BOSS:** I am very disinclined to do this. You are a lawyer and really need to be available to support your businesspeople if they have a question or need you.
>
> **NANCY:** I already cleared it with them and they are supportive. If I need to come in or be available on Fridays, I will be there for my clients.

BOSS: We have legal group staff meetings every other Friday morning.

NANCY: I will call into these and can also come in person for them when requested or where needed. How about we try it out; what do we have to lose? Say, for three months? At that time we can regroup, reassess, and see how it's working out.

BOSS: Okay, that sounds like a reasonable way to go.

After the three months were up, this was made a permanent arrangement. Asking "How about we try it out; what do we have to lose?" resulted in Nancy gaining the priceless benefit of being able to spend much more time with her infant and toddler children. The success of the question depended on her making a low-risk offer (she'd be available when needed on Fridays) that could very easily be undone by her simply going back to working a five-day week.

A final note about "How about we try it out; what do we have to lose?" A modified version of this question can be quite effective if you are the seller of a product or service and offer a money-back guarantee. In this case the question would be "With the money-back guarantee, you can return it for a full refund if you don't like it and you have have nothing to lose, so why not try it out?" One of the reasons we back most of our products in our business with a money-back guarantee is so that we can used this extremely powerful question. Here's how a typical negotiation goes:

POTENTIAL CLIENT: I am thinking of signing up for your Directory of Medical File Review Consultants and want to know how much business I will get for my $395.

AUTHORS: I can't honestly tell you exactly how much you will generate. This is a brand-new product and different doctors will get different results. What I can tell you is that we 100 percent back up your listing with a money-back guarantee for nine full months. With the money-back guarantee, you can cancel and get a full refund if you don't like it and you have nothing to lose, so why not try it out?

POTENTIAL CLIENT: Okay, I'll give it a try. I guess I have nothing to lose.

Lesson

"How about we try it for a while; what do we have to lose?" is a very effective question because it is so inherently reasonable. To give this question its best chance of success you should propose something that really is low risk. You should also be prepared to be flexible if the person you are negotiating with has legitimate concerns. This question is best used in nonadversarial negotiations with colleagues, business associates, and family members. A modified version of this question ("With the money-back guarantee, you can return it for a full refund if you don't like it and you have nothing to lose, so why not try it out?") can be quite effective for sellers of products or services backed by money-back guarantees.

How to Respond If You Are Asked "How about we try it for a while; what do we have to lose?"

This is an extremely reasonable question that is most often asked by a colleague. There are two main ways to respond to this question. The first is to agree to try it out. Usually this is best done by specifying the length, terms, and other details of the trial. This way, everybody is on the same page as to what the trial will consist of. For example, "Okay, we'll try out the new product. If we don't get twenty doctors to sign up by June 1, we'll agree that this has failed and pull the plug. Agreed?" If you cannot in good conscience agree to try out the proposal, then you must politely but firmly decline. The key to being able to do this and still maintain a good relationship with the other party is to be able to present powerful and persuasive reasons why there actually would be something to lose if this was tried out. For example, "Nancy, I can't agree to try this out. I have three other young mothers on my staff. If I let you do this, I'd have to let everyone do this, and then we'd have no coverage on Fridays. I'm very sorry about this. I wish I could agree."

Question #25

WHAT IF WE [INCREASED THE LENGTH OF DEAL/SIZE OF ORDER]?

Success in negotiation depends on careful listening. Success also depends on choosing your own words equally carefully. "What if" is a very effectively worded question for buyers to use to find out how much flexibility the seller has and also to help gain other valuable concessions. The subtext of the question is a powerful one: Better terms could result in a potentially lucrative long-term deal or bigger deal. The reasons that this question works include:

- It can broaden the scope of a proposed deal by making more generous terms a realistic possibility.

- You are not taking anything away from the table.

- It is usually safe to assume that the person you are negotiating with is interested in a bigger or longer-term deal.

- You have not committed yourself to additional terms.

- The question is a trial balloon designed to gauge the level of interest of the person you are negotiating with and to gain valuable information.

"What if we [increased the length of deal/size of order]?" is well worded since it dangles possibilities in front of the person you are negotiating with without you committing yourself to anything. For example, let's say you were to ask, "What if we were to make it a three-year deal?" Because of the wording of the question, you are not necessarily offering the three-year deal. You are merely asking how the terms would change if you were both able to do a three-year deal.

Any question that implies that you might be able to increase the size of your purchase or the length of your relationship is going to put you in a stronger negotiating position. One of the biggest carrots a negotiator can use is dangling the possibility of more work. This makes you a potentially far more valuable client or customer. As such, the person you are negotiating with will be motivated to do what it takes to land you and keep you happy. He has too much at stake to fail.

The response you receive to "What if we [increased the length of deal/size of order]?" should be carefully listened to since it can contain very valuable information as to how low the person you are negotiating with really can go on price or what other concessions can be made. For example, if you asked, "What if we were to make it a two-year deal?" and the person you are negotiating with answers, "Well, then we could do $85 a month, not $95 a month," you would then know that the person you are negotiating with can still make a profit at $85 a month and, therefore, has room to come down on his price. Better yet, since you haven't technically offered $95 a month you can still try to negotiate for the $85-a-month price.

As a fallback, and if necessary, you could always agree to a longer-term deal if that's what it takes to get your price.

The best time to ask "What if we [increased the length of deal/size of order]?" is when the negotiation has deadlocked over price or another key term. Asking this question at this time will almost always result in some conditional movement from the person you are negotiating with. Here's an example of how we have recently used this question:

> **TOTE BAG DISTRIBUTOR:** I can offer you the one thousand bags for $10 each, and that is my rock-bottom price.
>
> **AUTHORS (PURCHASER):** What if we bought five thousand bags?
>
> **TOTE BAG DISTRIBUTOR:** If you bought five thousand bags I could reduce the price to $8, payable within thirty days.
>
> **AUTHORS (PURCHASER):** We need to stick to the one thousand to start. If this works out, we expect to be ordering many thousands of bags for many years to come. The last vendor we used we ordered over fifteen thousand bags from in our five-plus years of doing business. If you can do $8, you've got yourself a deal.
>
> **TOTE BAG DISTRIBUTOR:** At one thousand bags, the best I can do is $8.50. I have certain fixed set-up costs that don't allow me to go lower on a run of that size.
>
> **AUTHORS (PURCHASER):** Done. I look forward to working together for many years to come.

As you can see from the above example, you should never underestimate the power and information to be gained from suggesting that if you are made happy you will be doing a lot more business in the future with the person you are negotiating with. Here we learned that $10 really was not the rock-bottom price it was claimed to be. Large orders and long-term relationships are very valuable to sellers. This fact can, and should, be used to your advantage.

Our business model is to develop long-term relationships. This saves us time and money. It also results in our getting great service and prices from our vendors since they don't want to lose us as customers.

When we put on conferences, we try to use the same hotels over and over again for this very reason. Negotiations with hotels often deadlock when we are asked to guarantee all of the hotel rooms, which our group may or may not use. This is standard in the vast majority of similar contracts, but we never sign such agreements. How can this be? Because we use the power of long-term relationships to our advantage and ask the right questions at the right time:

> **HOTEL:** I am sorry. I need you to guarantee all the sleeping rooms covered under the contract.
>
> **AUTHORS:** You understand that if something happens like the swine flu or a recession and the rooms aren't filled, we would be on the hook for tens of thousands of dollars of penalty fees?
>
> **HOTEL:** We need to protect ourselves, sir. That's our standard agreement and it's standard in the industry.
>
> **AUTHORS:** We never can, have, or will agree to this. It's a deal breaker. We only work with hotels interested in partnering with us for the long haul who understand our needs and value our business. Do you have Internet access there?
>
> **HOTEL:** Sure.
>
> **AUTHORS:** Please go to our Web site and click the tab "seminars." What you'll find is our seminar schedule for the last ten-plus years, which shows us using the same hotels over and over again. What if I were to tell you that if you removed that guarantee language from the contract it would be our intention to come to your property annually for the next ten years and generate millions of dollars of business for your hotel?
>
> **HOTEL:** Will you agree to a ten-year deal in writing?
>
> **AUTHORS:** I can't do that. I need you to continue to be motivated to do a good job and I have no idea what business con-

ditions will be like ten years—or even two years out. That said, our business model is to use the same hotels over and over. Every minute I spend looking for and negotiating with a new hotel I lose money. I want a place I can go back to for years. You have our history. If you would like us to consider your property, send us over a revised contract.

Floating the possibility of increasing the scope of the business dealings has been very effective for us. More times than not we are able to have the offending guarantee language removed. If we can't, we simply use another hotel that has greater long-term vision and will therefore be more accommodating.

Lesson

The possibility of an expanded business relationship can dramatically increase your negotiating power. "What if we [increased the length of deal/size of order]?" can be a simple way to help get a lower price or other favorable terms from a seller. The question itself is carefully worded in that it does not technically commit you to anything. The response to "What if we [increased the length of deal/size of order]?" will likely help you to see the additional concessions you might be able to get from the seller. This question is best used well into the negotiations when those negotiations have deadlocked over price or some other key terms.

How to Respond If You Are Asked "What if we [increased the length of deal/size of order]?"

This question is best answered with a question of your own. Namely, "Are you offering to sign a ten-year contract?" If the answer to your question is "yes," then you can and should consider additional inducements specifically and explicitly conditioned on a bigger deal. If the answer to your question is "no," then you should respond with something like, "Well, if you're not offering to sign a ten-year contract, can you agree to assure us of your future business?" The key here is not to agree to giving lower pricing without a firm commitment or condition that the deal will be expanded.

PART VII

The Right Price

INTRODUCTION: Price and terms of payment will obviously be an important issue in many negotiations. This section provides questions specifically designed to help you obtain better prices and payment terms.

Question #26

HOW MUCH FLEXIBILITY DO YOU HAVE IN THE PRICE?

When asking questions during a negotiation it's important to remember that it's not just what you are asking, it's *how* you are asking the question. One of the keys to the effective use of questions in negotiating is the precise way the question is phrased. A poorly phrased question can alienate the recipient or inadvertently push him into a corner. A well-phrased question can help the questioner to obtain critical information and also lead the recipient into an expected and helpful response.

The experienced negotiator understands that asking a pricing question in different ways may well lead to completely different answers and much poorer results in the negotiation. For example, if you ask the question "Is your price firm?" the answer will almost always be "yes." Here the recipient is forced into a "yes" or "no" response with little wiggle room. The authors' experience is that when forced into a corner with this type of question the recipient will often choose the wrong answer and just reply, "Yes, it is firm." This type of negative reply puts both parties into an untenable negotiating posture. The questioner may have to call into question the honesty of the recipient to make any progress. The recipient may have to admit that he was less than truthful or made a mistake. Making progress in the negotiation may be difficult.

Alternatively, if the question is worded, "Do you have any flexibility in your price?" many of the same issues are raised. This is again perceived as a "yes" or "no" question. The authors' experience is that almost all of the replies will be no, leaving the parties to find innovative ways to continue the negotiation.

When the question is phrased "How much flexibility do you have in the price?" the answer is invariably the same: "Not too much." This is the response that the questioner is looking for. It opens the subject of price up for discussion and the parties are left to negotiate how much money the buyer will be saving.

The question "How much flexibility do you have in the price?" is intended to:

- Gently remind the recipient that this is a negotiation, that is, a give-and-take, so it would make sense for him to leave himself room to negotiate.

- Put the recipient on the spot and have him admit that he has flexibility.

- Gain the person who asked the question information from the way the recipient answers the question:
  - Reluctantly
  - Too rapidly
  - With a grimace
  - Evasively
  - Honestly and openly
  - Dishonestly

One great advantage of asking "How much flexibility do you have in the price?" is that the response you receive will give you an immediate and clear indication of how invested the recipient is in getting the deal done. Of course, the more invested he is, the better it is for you since he won't want to let a deal he has invested time and effort in fall apart.

The thought process that the recipient of this simple and direct question goes through will probably include:

- **This is a fair question that should be answered.**

- **If I say I have no flexibility, I may be boxing myself in a corner and end up losing the deal.**

- **Saying I have no flexibility is not truthful and will cost me my credibility in the negotiation.**

- **If I have to back away later from a negative response, that will call into question my honesty and cause anything that I say during the negotiation to be questioned.**

- **The safest response to this direct and simple question is an honest reply that does not result in me having to give up too much.**

We successfully use this question on an ongoing basis. Like any good businesspeople, we need to spend money in order to make money. In our line of work, that means negotiating with countless vendors and service providers. Consistently asking this one question, "How much flexibility do you have in the price?" has probably saved us at least 5 percent in expenses over the years, translating directly to hundreds of thousands of dollars of additional profits.

———

Here's a specific example. Many years ago, we were producing an educational videotape and needed to hire a video production company to do the filming and editing. Here's how the negotiation went.

AUTHORS: I want your price for shooting a video in your studio. We will be doing mostly talking heads with very little graphics. We are looking for two 8-hour days in your studio and asking that you supply the director and the equipment.

PRODUCTION COMPANY (VENDOR): Well it all depends on how many bells and whistles you want.

AUTHORS: We will not be filming *Star Wars* here. It will be two to three professionals reading from a teleprompter and about forty-five pages of script. The talent are pros and have been here before. Can you give me a price or should I go down the street to get this filmed?

PRODUCTION COMPANY (VENDOR): We are reluctant to bid out jobs without specific specs in writing, but you are looking at $50,000 here for a first-rate job

AUTHORS: I appreciate your frankness and we would love to do business with you on account of your reputation, but your price is very high.

PRODUCTION COMPANY (VENDOR): Quality work is not cheap. . . . You can probably go down to a film school and get some students who are doing work study to film it for a lot less if you didn't care much about quality.

AUTHORS: How much flexibility do you have in your price?

PRODUCTION COMPANY (VENDOR): Not too much . . . we have fixed costs here, and the staff likes to get paid occasionally.

AUTHORS: When you say "not too much," what are we talking about?

PRODUCTION COMPANY (VENDOR): I could . . . let's see . . . I could knock 15 percent off if you worked around our schedule.

By asking one simple question, "How much flexibility do you have in your price?" we were able to boost our bottom line by $7,500. Not bad for three seconds spent asking a question. Over the years, the savings realized from asking this simple yet artfully worded question have really added up.

Here's an additional fun example. When we were deciding on a publisher for this book we had discussions with interested editors from various publishing houses. In one of these meetings we were very pleased to hear that the editor we were dealing with had already started using the questions in our manuscript successfully. When we asked which question and under what circumstances she replied, "'How much flexibility do you have in your price?' I used it to get a $100 rent reduction from my landlord." That's $1,200 in savings over one year or $12,000 in savings over ten years. An excellent rate of return for asking one question.

Lesson

Asking the question "How much flexibility do you have in your price?" will frequently open up the discussion of price and save you money. As with many of the questions we describe, always remember that the precise wording of the question may be critical. For example, asking "Do you have any flexibility in the price?" will likely result in a negative response, which will impede the negotiation and cost you money.

How to Respond If You Are Asked "How much flexibility do you have in the price?"

A good way to respond to this question is to condition your price flexibility on a concession from the buyer. For example, "If you were to sign a two-year lease I can knock $100 per month off the lease," or, "If you were to pay cash and buy today I can knock $200 off the price." In this way you are both showing flexibility in your price, but at the same time conditioning this flexibility on a valuable concession from the other side.

Question #27

ARE YOU INTERESTED IN QUALITY OR PRICE?

This is a question for sellers. The person you are negotiating with will often object to your offered price when you are trying to sell something. When the price objection is made, you will be much more likely to prevail on price if you can convince the person you are negotiating with that your product or service is of superior quality. Asking "Are you interested in quality or price?" is a shrewd way to move the person you are negotiating with away from thinking about price (which disfavors you) and toward the quality of your product or services (which favors you).

"Are you interested in quality or price?" is extremely well designed since it will move the focus of the negotiations to your turf (i.e., quality) in a way where you do not appear to be pushy, desperate, or giving a typical sales job. The subtexts of the question are quite powerful, namely: The buyer can have high quality or low price, but not both. You, the seller, have quality. Quality is worth a premium. The buyer gets what he pays for, and if the buyer is looking for a cheap piece of crap, he can certainly find that somewhere else.

The reasons that "Are you interested in quality or price?" is effective include:

- It forces the person you are negotiating with to admit (tacitly or outright) that you have a high-quality product or service.

- It subtly reinforces the idea that it makes little sense to want both the highest quality and the lowest price.

- It can often gain an admission from the person that you are negotiating with that they are in fact looking for a high-quality product or service.

- It serves as a reminder that high-quality products/ services deliver results in line with their higher prices.

The best time to ask "Are you interested in quality or price?" is when the person you are negotiating with starts to complain about the price you have demanded. He is likely to respond in one of the following ways:

- I want both.

- We are willing to pay for high quality, within reason.

- Can you prove your claims to high quality?

- Will the initial higher price pay off in terms of results, longevity, fewer service problems, etc.?

- How can I justify the higher price to my superiors?

- How much better is your product or service?

- How much of a price differential would I be paying?

Your response to each of these objections should be a focus on quality, value, and an explanation of why you have to charge the price you are offering. Quality can focus on longevity, additional features, and other real benefits. The point of your value arguments should be long-term and total cost. Why you have to charge so much should again focus on value—how things in your product or service that are of benefit to the buyer cost money.

If the person you are negotiating with replies that he is just looking for the cheapest price, you still have some cards to play. A good course of action in this case is to recommend some cheap alternative and where this can be obtained. When you do so, point out the features, missing benefits, and hidden costs that make the competing product or service in actuality a poor value.

It goes without saying that "Are you interested in quality or price?" is best used where you are well prepared to explain the value in your product. You will be well positioned to use this question if you work hard to create valuable products and services. Equally important is being able to articulate this value clearly. The buyer needs to be able to understand and explain to his supervisors that in the long run they will save more money or make more money by going with your higher-quality product or service.

Our business philosophy is simple. If we do not truly believe in a product or service's value, we won't sell it. Because we focus obsessively on value and quality, we are able to use "Are you interested in quality or price?" all the time when clients balk at paying the prices we charge.

Here's a typical example. Part of our business involves selling products, training, and services to expert witnesses. After many requests we decided to create a detailed, standard contract, which expert witnesses can use when lawyers are looking to hire them. The contract is four pages long. We sell it for $150. Every once in a while we get a client who balks at paying $150 *for four pages*. In addition, why pay us all this money if they have either never used a written contract or have been using for years something they (non-lawyers) drafted themselves?

PURCHASER: I am looking at your company's Expert Witness Retention Contract on your Web site. It is $150. How many printed pages is it?

AUTHORS: It is approximately four pages.

PURCHASER: Isn't that a little steep for four pages? Like more than $35 a page?

AUTHORS: Are you interested in quality or price?

PURCHASER: I want both.

AUTHORS: Well, you can certainly draft your own, go without a written contract, or find something free on the Internet, but I wouldn't recommend it. Two highly experienced attorneys whose sole legal focus is expert witnessing worked 100-plus hours to draft our contract. That's twenty-five hours per page. We receive numerous calls each week from experts who have been screwed over left and right by lawyers and the system. Each time we received a call like this we added language in the contract to protect the expert from having that problem happen to them. In addition, the contract was peer reviewed by high-powered experts, trial attorneys, and judges. The contract prevents innumerable serious, potentially career-ending problems and difficulties. I get weekly calls from clients telling me how much money the contract has saved them and the countless potential horror stories it has prevented. These are people earning $50,000 to $100,000-plus per year from expert witnessing who want nothing less than bulletproof protection. We offer a thirty-day money-back guarantee. Over 900 people have purchased the contract and we've only received three or four back for returns.

PURCHASER: Do you offer any discounts?

AUTHORS: I am sorry, we do not.

PURCHASER: Okay, I'll take it. Can I give you my credit card number?

Consider another example. As discussed in Question #22, one of the authors was helping his elderly uncle shop for a new car a few years back. Previous to negotiating the price, he had to be convinced which car he wanted to buy. He was down to choosing between a Ford sedan and a Honda Accord. Here's how the conversation went with the Honda dealer (who had an excellent salesperson).

BUYER: Okay, I like the car, but the Ford is $3,000 less expensive. I'm a retired teacher, you know. On a fixed income.

SALESPERSON Are you interested in quality or price?

BUYER: Both.

SALESPERSON: You should look at the total cost of ownership. The better value is clearly with the Accord. You'll spend far less time in the shop, it is far more likely to run longer, and above all, your resale value is going to be much, much higher with the Accord. You also have a far more fuel-efficient design and more creature comforts. I had a guy go with the American brand about a year ago, and I lost the deal since we couldn't meet their price. Just last week, he traded it in to me and got an Accord. He told me that he should have listened to me in the first place.

BUYER: Okay, you convinced me. Let's talk more about price on the Honda. Are you aware that another Honda dealer is charging a lot less?

Lesson

"Are you interest in quality or price?" is a well-designed question that will focus the negotiation toward the quality of your product. It is best used when the person you are negotiating with complains about your price. To best position yourself to use this question you should sell products or services of superior quality. You should also be very well prepared to articulate the superior value of your products or services (e.g., how over the long term they will cost the customer less than the seemingly cheaper alternative).

How to Respond If You Are Asked "Are you interested in quality or price?"

"Are you interested in quality or price?" is designed to get you to buy into the premise that you can't have both quality and price. There is no reason that you need to buy into such a limiting premise. Accordingly, a good answer to this question is "I am interested in, and frankly deserve, both quality *and* price." Alternatively, a little flattery might help the negotiating process. For example, "I wouldn't be talking with you if you did not have high-quality products, but price is crucial to my employer and for me. Do you want to sell your high-quality product to me today?"

Question #28

DO YOU WANT TO BE RICH OR FAMOUS?

When attempting to get someone to agree to do work for you or your company, most people wrongly assume it is always just about the money. This is because (as the old business adage says) we often do not see things as they are, we see things as we are.

It's always a serious negotiating mistake to assume we know entirely what the other party wants. The experienced and successful negotiator understands that there are a whole host of things that people want, all of which can drive a negotiation. These include:

- **More time with their family**

- **Respect**

- **Recognition**

- **Long-term relationships**

- **Publicity**

- To be liked

- Fame

- To help out someone or something

- To look like a hero

- Money

The question "Do you want to be rich or famous?" is a simple and direct way to get the person you are negotiating with to open up and talk about his needs, interests, and desires. The question is nonthreatening, can be taken as friendly or humorous, and can easily seduce the person at whom it is targeted to open up. In fact, the lighthearted way the question is asked tends to catch the recipient off guard. As the question does not seem too serious or important revealing responses are common.

Determining what the person you are negotiating with really wants can save you huge amounts of money, help you determine your best negotiating approach, and help you achieve a win-win agreement where both parties are very satisfied.

We routinely ask this question of people whom we're looking to work with. Although it's counterintuitive, many people are *not* interested in the money but are, in fact, more interested in something else, such as spending more time with their family, helping a good cause, being able to travel more, etc. Meeting those nonmonetary needs has resulted in many successful negotiations and has saved the authors hundreds of thousands of dollars over the years.

Let's look at an example. A few years ago, we were coauthoring a complex medical-legal textbook. We wanted to have a physician read and review the textbook to see if we had made any technical

or scientific errors. We selected a physician to approach for reviewing the text. The problem was that the physician we selected
was very accomplished and could reasonably ask for $500 an hour
for his work. The review of the 500-page book could take a hundred hours or more. So the review process could end up costing
us $50,000.

We approached the physician with the project anyway, and he
said he was interested, so we sent him the book. Instead of asking
him how much he would charge us, we asked him, "Do you want
to be rich or famous?" His reply was very revealing. He stated that
he was *not* interested in the money. He really liked the book,
thought he could improve it, and instead of money wanted to be a
coauthor. He revealed that he wanted to burnish his academic
résumé and thought this book would help him. This was truly a
win-win negotiation result. The physician got exactly what he asked
for and was very pleased with the result. We received, in return, a
thoroughly reviewed manuscript (the fact that the physician was
a coauthor gave him even more incentive to do a truly excellent
job), a well-known physician as a coauthor, which helped us to
market the textbook successfully, and it cost us nothing to add
his name to the book (the physician reviewer received no fee and
no royalties).

Some of you are probably thinking, "Well, what if he said he
wanted to be rich, what would you have done?" While this is not
the common response, this has happened on occasion. Here is how
we have dealt with that response.

The authors wanted to ask a high-powered expert to speak at one of
our conferences. When we informed him that we do not pay our
speakers, he was reluctant to commit to the conference. We asked
him the same simple question, "Do you want to be rich or famous?"
He replied, "I want to be rich." We explained that we send out more
than one million pieces of direct mail for our conferences each year.

He would have his picture in one of the brochures, with his bio and contact information.

We further explained to him that what was likely to happen was that his profile in his profession would dramatically increase, he would gain national recognition, and lucrative consulting opportunities would make themselves available to him. His conclusion (you are always better letting the recipient reach his own conclusion if possible) was that the best way to get rich was to speak for us. The speaking engagement did in the end lead to numerous very lucrative consulting opportunities, and resulted in a long-term relationship with us that continues to this day.

Another potentially ideal time to use a variation of this question is when you're buying a house. When buying a house, getting the absolute highest price may *not* be the seller's prime concern. Some sellers will accept a lower bid if the buyers are more likely to get financing or the timing of the closing is accommodating. Asking a seller's agent a good question like "Do they (the sellers) want top dollar or are they looking for a quick, smooth, and certain transaction?" can yield surprising and invaluable information.

Lesson

"Do you want to be rich or famous?" (or a variation thereof) is a very effective negotiation question regardless of how the recipient answers because it gives you an invaluable insight into your opponent's mind-set and desires.

How to Respond If You Are Asked "Do you want to be rich or famous?"

One way to answer this question is to lightheartedly respond, "I'd like to be both. Who wouldn't?" This response is believable and does not provide the other person with any information that can be used against you. Alternatively, you can answer with a request for more details about both alternatives. For example, "I like the sound of both rich and famous. . . . Can you run through both scenarios for me to help me decide?" This gives you more information and time to make an informed choice.

Question #29

HOW MUCH DO YOU ESTIMATE
THAT WILL COME OUT TO?

Many of the questions in this book are designed to be used in a wide variety of circumstances. This is not one of them. "How much do you estimate that will come out to?" is designed to flesh out pie-in-the-sky, hard-to-figure-out, speculative or contingent promises made by the person you are negotiating with. Once you get this person to come up with a hard number, you can anchor him to this figure and negotiate for a more solid and advantageous compensation formula.

Oftentimes during negotiations you will be promised results or compensation based on a formula left to the discretion of the person you are negotiating with. This can end up being a nightmarish scenario for you. Here's a quick example. Many, many years ago, one of the authors was hired into a new job at a small firm and was verbally promised 10 percent of the profits of the firm. Here's about how the negotiations went:

AUTHOR: How much is the compensation you are offering
EMPLOYER: $42,500 a year salary *plus* 10 percent of the

profits of the firm. As you know we are a nicely profitable firm.

AUTHOR: This sounds great. When can I start?

To make a long story short, the author never saw a dime of profit money. After the author was hired, the employer and his partner dramatically increased their own salaries such that expenses went up dramatically and all profits were eliminated.

The profit figure was easily manipulated by the employer. As such, this turned out to be a phantom bonus worth almost nothing. Ever since this day, we the authors have been very leery of compensation that is not fixed, transparent, or is open to manipulation by the other party. Had we to do it over, here's how the negotiation with the employer would have gone:

AUTHOR: How much is the compensation you are offering?

EMPLOYER: $42,500 a year salary *plus* 10 percent of the profits of the firm.

AUTHOR: How much do you estimate that will come out to?

EMPLOYER: Here are our financials. Our profit has been $150,000 to $250,000 and generally increasing annually.

AUTHOR: So your expectation is that I will be paid bonuses of $15,000 to $25,000 a year or more?

EMPLOYER: Exactly.

AUTHOR: As you know, profits can easily vary through accounting methods, increase in expenses, etc. I see here that your firm grossed approximately $1,500,000 in each of the past five years. If you make my bonus 1.5 percent of the *gross* of your firm, you've got yourself a new team member.

"How much do you estimate that will come out to?" is very effective at smoking out real offers of compensation and results from illusory ones. The idea is to pin the person you are negotiating with down to estimating a figure. Since they are claiming that this is such a good deal for you, you are subtly encouraging them to come up with a high figure. Once they state the high figure, you then need to negotiate an alternative arrangement where it is much more likely that you will actually receive what you need for the deal to make sense.

Another nice thing about "How much do you estimate that will come out to?" is that the question has almost no downside. Simply put, nothing bad is likely to result from asking this question. As such, it should be routinely used in situations where you are offered compensation or benefits that you fear may be illusory.

We use "How much do you estimate that will come out to?" all the time in our training business. What usually happens is that a professional organization will want to hire us to train their members at an annual meeting. We are usually offered "50 percent of profits." This is a nonstarter for us since, as we have seen above, profits can so easily be manipulated. Here are how the negotiations typically go:

> **PROFESSIONAL ORGANIZATION:** We'd like you to fly out from Boston to San Francisco and spend the day training the members of our association. We can offer you equal partnership, that is 50 percent of the profits from the meeting.
> **AUTHORS:** How much do you estimate that will come out to?
> **PROFESSIONAL ORGANIZATION:** $20,000.
> **AUTHORS:** How many people are you expecting?
> **PROFESSIONAL ORGANIZATION:** Fifty to a hundred.
> **AUTHORS:** What is the per-head tuition?
> **PROFESSIONAL ORGANIZATION:** $500.
> **AUTHORS:** We can do it for a $15,000 flat fee.

PROFESSIONAL ORGANIZATION: We can't agree to that—what if we don't get our numbers? We'd lose our shirts.

AUTHORS: Well, since you were expecting fifty to a hundred people and to pay us $5,000 more than this, you should make out much better under these circumstances. To hedge your bets, however, we can put in a clause that states that you can cancel this agreement without penalty thirty days out from the meeting date if you don't have at least fifty people signed up to date.

PROFESSIONAL ORGANIZATION: That works for us.

Notice how effective "How much do you estimate that will come out to?" was in pinning down the organization. They were encouraged to answer with a high number since they were trying to entice us to agree to their proposal. We used their own high number against them in a way that protected us from the possibility of performing many hours of hard work for little or no compensation.

One final example. A few years ago, we were approached by a company that wanted to digitize one of our books and make this content available to consumers electronically. We were skeptical of the business model but were at least offered a royalty based on gross revenues and not "profits." The problem was that setting the whole process up would eat up valuable time on our end and we needed to find out if this was likely to be worth our while. Here's how the negotiation went:

ELECTRONIC PUBLISHER: We are offering a 10 percent royalty on gross sales of the electronic version of your book.

AUTHORS: How much do you estimate that will come out to?

ELECTRONIC PUBLISHER: Well, we are estimating that your royalties would be at least $20,000 over the next three years.

AUTHORS: If you give us a nonrefundable, guaranteed $10,000 advance on royalties payable over the next three years, you've got yourself a deal.

ELECTRONIC PUBLISHER: We can do $7,500—$2,500 per year.

AUTHORS: Done.

Note how we used the publisher's own prediction against him. "How much do you estimate that will come out to?" encouraged the high $20,000 figure that was used since the publisher was enticing us to agree to their proposal. In the end, the electronic version of the book did not earn royalties even close to the advance. The result, of course, is that "How much do you estimate that will come out to?" made us a significant amount of money that we otherwise would have lost.

Lesson

You should be very cautious when you are offered compensation or other benefits that are hard to pin down, speculative, or could be easily manipulated to your disadvantage after the fact by the person you are negotiating with. If you are confronted with such an offer you should as a rule ask "How much do you estimate that will come out to?" There is no downside risk to asking this question. The person you are negotiating with will be motivated to suggest a large number. Once you have this number, use it as an anchor and negotiate a more certain and advantageous arrangement.

How to Respond If You Are Asked "How much do you estimate that will come out to?"

The person asking this question is trying to pin you down and anchor you to a firm number that will then be used against you. In light of this, a good way to answer this question is to provide a vague answer or to tactfully dodge the question. For example, "Well, that depends on our revenue and expenses. There's no absolute guarantee on either, of course." Or, "There's no way to know for sure; it all depends what transpires between now and then." Alternatively, you can tie it back to the questioner by stating, "That will depend on the quality of your work and performance. You do have confidence in your ability to perform, don't you?" This will put the questioner on the defensive and correctly point out that what you are negotiating is pay for performance.

Question #30

WILL YOU GIVE US A BEST-PRICE GUARANTEE?

People are usually very simple in what they want. They only want the best. In negotiating, one way to get the best possible deal is to ask for it. Asking "Will you give us a best-price guarantee?" can be a simple and effective way to help ensure a great deal.*

This is a very helpful question to ask partly because of its many subtexts. By asking this question you will communicate clearly that price is of crucial concern to you and that you are not in a rush. You are also communicating pretty clearly that you are shopping around and that the failure to obtain a great price will likely result in a lost sale. All of these messages will help you build negotiating leverage and obtain a better deal.

Asking "Will you give us a best-price guarantee?" can easily put the person you are negotiating with in a tight spot since a "no" answer will likely appear blatantly unreasonable and almost always result in a lost sale. The person you are negotiating with is, therefore, left with the choice of either making the guarantee or somehow

* As you will see below, best-price guarantees can come in different forms.

sweetening the deal to get around the question. All of these results are positive for you. Even if the answer is a simple "no," you've learned that you should probably not be dealing with this person or company.

When using this question, you should always try to put yourself in the shoes of the person you are negotiating with. This question will really get him thinking. When you ask, "Will you give us a best-price guarantee?" the person you are negotiating with will have to rapidly consider many things, including:

- Is my price in fact the best price I offer and that competitors offer?

- How transparent should I be concerning his other arrangements/deals?

- Would I have to renegotiate with all my other customers?

- Is there a confidentiality issue involved?

- Can I do this even if I wanted to?

- What if the proponent of the question already has become aware of a better price from the recipient?

- Would an explicit or implicit refusal to answer the question demonstrate that they are not getting the best price? What about other factors such as service, shipping, delivery, warranty, etc.? Maybe I can get around this by sweetening the deal in this area so we are comparing apples to our competitor's oranges.

- How would the guarantee work (i.e., how long would it last, what would be the mechanics of such an arrangement)?

- What precedential value would this set for future negotiation with this customer? How would I protect myself from the person I am negotiating from revealing the price and even worse, the guarantee to others?

- What legal issues are raised by this guarantee?

- Would I have to have my superiors sign off on this arrangement? If so, what are they likely to say when I raise the issue?

The sum total result of these questions is more negotiating leverage for you.

The final merit to "Will you give us a best-price guarantee?" is the fact that there is really no downside to asking this question. Although some of the negotiating questions described here pose some risk of backfiring, this is not one of them. As such, it can and should probably be used in many if not most negotiations.

As with many of the questions described in this book, the timing of when you ask it is important. The most effective time to ask the question is when the person you are negotiating with has essentially assured you that you are getting the best price. It should not be too difficult to steer him into such an assertion by asking something like "Is this the best price out there?" or "Is this the best price you will offer in the next thirty days?" or something similar. Once he is set up and answers affirmatively, it is then time to ask the question "Will you give us a best-price guarantee?"

Body language and voice tone should also be closely watched. When the person you are negotiating with responds, consider not just what they say, but how they say it. Do they look as though they are confident that you are getting the best price or do they look disappointed and unsettled by your question? If the reaction is the latter, you might be best off continuing to shop around.

Let's consider a couple of examples. One of the authors' wives is an investment management lawyer. Part of her job is to negotiate fees with money managers. (Money managers typically charge an annual percentage of the value of the assets that they manage.) As part of these negotiations, she would as a rule ask for a best-price guarantee, namely that her client would be not be charged more than any of the money manager's other clients. Furthermore, if the money manager during the term of the agreement lowered his rates for any other client, he would have to lower his rates for her client as well. Such "most favored nation" clauses were very commonly obtained and resulted in saving her client and her client's investors tens of millions of dollars in fees.

Our business sends out a good deal of mail. A few years ago, we were negotiating for a new piece of equipment to help process our outgoing mail. As you can see from the following example, asking "Will you give us a best-price guarantee?" was very helpful in us obtaining a great deal. The negotiation went something like this:

AUTHORS: We are looking for an excellent price for the folding machine.
VENDOR: Understood. I have already cut $1,200 off the list price.
AUTHORS: The price of $7,900 is still pretty steep. What is your best price?
VENDOR: $7,500 if you purchase it today!
AUTHORS: Does your company sell this for less than $7,500?
VENDOR: Nobody can purchase it for less than $7,500.
AUTHORS: Will you give me a written best-price guarantee?

VENDOR: What specifically are you looking for?

AUTHORS: Just an e-mail guaranteeing this is the lowest price the folding machine is sold for and 120 percent of the difference if and when we find a lower price within the next six months or you sell one to anybody else at a lower price in the next six months.

VENDOR: I hear you, I do, but this is something we just aren't capable of doing. We stand by our prices, but I can't control what other people might do. Maybe they are putting something on clearance? Maybe they are selling as a loss leader? Let me talk to my boss and get back to you.

The next day we got a call back.

VENDOR: Here's what we came up with and this is as far as we can go. $7,300 is the best possible price we can do. We will also give you a written guarantee that we will not sell this machine for less to anybody else in the next ninety days. If we do, we will automatically refund you 110 percent of the difference. In addition, we will throw in a free one-year extension on your warranty, which is worth over $500.

AUTHORS: We appreciate your making this work for us. You've got yourself a deal.

Notice that although we didn't get everything we had asked for, we were able to obtain an even better deal than their previous "best" offer. We accepted their reasons for not being able to guarantee what other people might do since they made sense to us. The tone and language of their response also indicated to us that they appeared to be doing the best they could on price. Note: Had they responded "no" without any explanation or sweetener, we would have walked away from the deal and kept shopping around since we would have strongly suspected that there were better deals to be had.

Lesson

Asking "Will you give us a best-price guarantee?" is a low-risk way to help yourself to obtain the best possible deal. This question is best used after the person you are negotiating with has already given his best price. After asking this question you will usually either be provided with the guarantee, another valuable concession, or an indication that you should keep shopping around.

How to Respond If You Are Asked "Will you give us a best-price guarantee?"

There are different ways to answer this question. If your business model is to beat any competitor's price, then your answer to this question is a confident "Absolutely." Of course, this response leaves the terms and details of the guarantee vague. You would want to negotiate these as favorably as possible. If you choose not to give the guarantee you will need a reasonable response. One way to do so is to assert that your product or service is unique. For example, "Nobody else is offering the quality service that we do. We can't compete with low-end providers." In this situation the other party is likely to respond that they want the best price you give any of your past, present, or future customers (a "most favored nation" clause). This is a more difficult request to deny. The best way to do so is to point to legal, regulatory, or accounting difficulties, and reply with a statement such as, "I'm sorry, because of confidentiality and legal concerns and because the information is proprietary, we are not allowed to discuss confidential pricing for other clients. You would not want us to reveal your information after you become a client."

Question #31

WHAT IF I WERE TO PAY CASH?

Cash is king. In many, many circumstances a significantly better deal can be obtained if the buyer agrees to pay cash. Asking "What if I were to pay cash?" is a simple and easy way to see if additional concessions can be obtained by paying cash. The subtext of the question is simple: If you can make additional concessions, I might agree to pay in cash.

Many people like to get paid in cash. Some people *love* to get paid in cash. Small-business owners and self-employed persons such as contractors are traditionally most fond of being paid in cash.

Cash eliminates from the seller's expense side what can be hefty credit-card processing fees (these can go up to around 3.5 percent). Cash eliminates uncertainties as to whether a proffered check will bounce. Cash is simple to use and does not require any infrastructure or resources to process payment. Cash is immediately available for use by the seller. Cash saves a trip to the bank that would be required with a check.

In order to best use this question, we suggest that you first negotiate a good price with the explicit agreement that the seller will take a check or credit card as payment. Only after you have obtained a good price should you ask, "What if I were to pay cash?" In many circumstances, especially where dealing with a self-employed person or small-business owner, you will be able to obtain significant extra concessions for paying cash. Where cash is used as a form of payment you will, of course, want to get a signed receipt as proof of payment.

"What if I were to pay cash?" is a nice question to use since it is very low risk once you have already established that other forms of payment are acceptable. By asking "What if I were to pay cash?" you are not committing yourself to anything. You are merely floating a trial balloon. If the benefits offered back are good enough you can agree to a cash deal and save a good deal of money. If they are not, you can just pay in a different way (check or charge) as had been previously discussed.

Living within your means and keeping a good cash reserve can put you in a stronger bargaining position. In order to be able to use "What if I were to pay cash?" you obviously need to have access to enough cash for the purchase. We have been able to use our ability and willingness to pay cash to save large amounts of money over the years. Here are some examples.

One of the authors recently negotiated with an electrician to have some work done on his house. Here's how the conversation went:

> **AUTHOR:** We're looking for you to wire cable in three additional rooms.
> **ELECTRICIAN:** Okay, I charge time and materials. Time is $80 a hour.
> **AUTHOR:** I need a firm price.
> **ELECTRICIAN:** $1,000.
> **AUTHOR:** When would you hope to start?
> **ELECTRICIAN:** Couple of weeks.

AUTHOR: You of course accept credit cards?

ELECTRICIAN: I prefer a check.

AUTHOR: Do you accept Visa?

ELECTRICIAN: Yes.

AUTHOR: What if I were to pay cash?

ELECTRICIAN: Well, we always prefer cash. For cash, I can do this for $800.

AUTHOR: Okay, done, $800 cash.

ELECTRICIAN: Perfect. I can start day after tomorrow if it's okay with you.

Notice how we first locked the electrician into a price based on a credit-card payment. The implication was that we needed to charge this, so his choice was take a credit card or lose the job. Only once the acceptability of credit-card payment was established did we float the trial balloon of paying cash. Cash payment turned out (as often is the case) to be very attractive to the electrician. We were able to save 20 percent and get the job done quickly.

In a similar vein, one of the authors recently used this technique when buying some diamond earrings for his daughter from a small, privately owned jewelry shop.

AUTHOR: What's the asking price on these?*

JEWELER: A beautiful pair, sir. Famous designer. $2,000.

AUTHOR: Are you the owner?

JEWELER: Yes.

AUTHOR: Your price is high. How much flexibility do you have in your price?

---

* Another good negotiating question because this pushes the other party to buy into the fact that the price is negotiable. This is much better than asking, "What's the price on these?"

JEWELER: Actually, we can do 25 percent off.

AUTHOR: $1,500?

JEWELER: Yes.

AUTHOR: That's still high. Would you take $1,250?

JEWELER: I can go as low as $1,400.

AUTHOR: I see on your window that you take AMEX. Is that right?

JEWELER: Yes.

AUTHOR: What if I were to pay cash?

JEWELER: Well, for cash we can do $1,150.

AUTHOR: Done, but I'll need a receipt.

JEWELER: With pleasure.

Effective use of "What if I were to pay cash?" requires laying the groundwork. In this example the groundwork was laid by establishing that this was a small business, confirming that I was dealing with the owner, negotiating a low price and confirming that credit card payment was acceptable. The net result of the cash question was a $250—or 17 percent—price concession.

"What if I were to pay cash?" was low risk in this situation. The worst the jeweler could have said was "no." At that point I could have walked away or taken the deal for $1,400 with AMEX as a payment. I would have been no worse off than before I had floated the cash trial balloon.

Here's another fun story. Many years ago, one of the authors was at an antique-book show in Boston. There were booksellers from all over the world. The author was very interested in a 400-year-old map taken from an antique Dutch book. The seller was a London antiquarian book dealer. Here's about how the negotiation went:

AUTHOR: I see you're asking $1,400 U.S. for this print?

BOOK DEALER: Right so.

AUTHOR: How much flexibility do you have in the price?

BOOK DEALER: I can come down to $1,200.

AUTHOR: What if we used Mr. Green?

BOOK DEALER: Mr. Green?

AUTHOR (TAKES OUT A WAD OF BILLS): Cash.

BOOK DEALER (WIDE EYES): Ah yes, Mr. Green. Bloody good. $700.

AUTHOR: Done.

Floating the idea of a cash transaction was able to gain a huge concession from the seller. There was no risk to this offer. We didn't commit ourselves to anything.

Cash can be king in other situations as well. A few years ago, one of the authors and his wife were negotiating to buy a house. They were able to buy the house even though they were not the high bidder. Since the author was offering to pay cash (with a bank check), the seller did not have to worry about the deal falling through if financing could not be obtained.

One final example. Many years ago, the authors were working with a video production company that was helping the authors produce some educational videotapes. Under the terms of a deal we had negotiated with our joint venture partner, we would receive $150,000 as soon as the videotapes were completed, so we were obviously quite eager to get the videos completed.

The problem was that the video production company was not being responsive. We could not get the company to schedule time in their one edit suite to get the videos edited. They wouldn't ask their editor to work on weekends to get this done since they didn't want to burn him out. We brainstormed many different ways to get them to do the work. We discussed suing them. We talked about firing them and starting from scratch with a new company. Nothing seemed likely to work. Finally, we agreed on a course of action we thought might work. We scheduled a five-minute meeting directly with the editor who we needed to do the work on a weekend. Here's about how it went:

> **AUTHOR:** We need this project done and we'd like you to come in this weekend to finish the editing.
> **EDITOR:** Gee, you know, that's not really ideal for me. I have to take the cat to the vet on Saturday. My in-laws are coming over on Sunday. Plus, there's some yard work to do.
> **AUTHOR (PULLS OUT WAD OF CASH):** You come in this weekend and get this done and we'll make it worth your while.
> **EDITOR (SMILING AND ENTHUSIASTIC):** I'll be in at 7:00 A.M. on Saturday.

The tapes were finished on Sunday and the editor received a nice cash tip for exceptional service. We received our $150,000 from our joint venture partner shortly thereafter.

Lesson

Cash is king. Many people love to get paid in cash and will make significant price concessions in order to receive cash as payment. Asking "What if I were to pay cash?" is a no-risk way to possibly gain significant price concessions. "What if I were to pay cash?" is best deployed to gain additional concessions after you have fixed a price and agreed on payment by means other than cash. To be able to use this question you will need to have access to the required amount of cash.

How to Respond If You Are Asked "What if I were to pay cash?"

There are three general ways to respond to this question. If cash is not a preferable payment option then your answer should be something like, "I would accept cash, yes." This is a nice way of saying that there will be no discount for payment in cash.

If, on the other hand, you would strongly prefer cash, it is appropriate to respond with a fitting inducement. One way to do so could be, "Cash will save me on my credit-card fees. If you pay cash today, I'm happy to take 2 percent off your total bill. Why make the banks rich? Let's both save some money."

If you and the other party have not previously covered terms of payment, there is another, riskier way to respond to this question. When someone asks this question, you can probably safely assume that they could pay cash if they wanted to. If you want to try to get a little aggressive you could respond, "The price I quoted *is* a cash price. I am happy to take a major credit card, but would have to add on a 3.5 percent convenience fee." This answer might just get you your original price paid in cash.

Question #32

YOU, OF COURSE, ACCEPT MAJOR CREDIT CARDS?

Price is not the only consideration in a buy/sell transaction. The form of payment can also be important. "You, of course, accept major credit cards?" is a good question to ask to make sure that you will be able to pay with a credit card.

It is usually to a buyer's advantage to pay with a credit card. The first advantage is rewards. The second advantage is float. The more time you have to pay something, the better off you are.

The advantages of using a rewards credit card can be quite significant. One of the authors has a rewards card in which 2 percent of every purchase gets deposited directly into an investment account. That's basically 2 percent cash back on each and every purchase. Because of this, we try to charge as many purchases as we can. (We always pay the bill off on time and never pay interest.) Over the years, and with investment returns, this has been worth thousands of free dollars.

The authors also run a midsize business. Wherever possible we negotiate to be able to pay with a credit card. There are a lot of expenses in a business like ours. Annually, we charge hundreds of thousands of dollars on our corporate credit cards. This has directly translated into numerous free rewards for travel, furniture, electronics, and other benefits.

The problem, of course, is that sellers prefer to get paid via cash, check, or electronic funds transfer. The reason for this is simple: Credit-card companies charge a fee to sellers of up to 3.5 percent of the sales total. If you are buying a pricey item, these fees can become very significant. As such, sellers strongly prefer that a buyer pay with cash or check.

Many times, a seller will state in their offer or on their literature that they accept credit cards. Many times, they won't. In these circumstances, you best negotiate this up front in order to make sure that the seller will accept a credit card as payment. Here's an example of how problems may arise. A few years ago, we hired a contractor to put in a sprinkler system. It was a $5,000 job. We charged $500 as a deposit to our credit card. When the job was completed and we were billed $4,500, we asked to charge the amount to our credit card. The vendor refused since this would likely cost him more than $100 in credit-card processing fees. After this experience, we now make it a point up front to settle on the form of payment. "You, of course, accept major credit cards?" is designed to deal with vendors like the sprinkler contractor.

We suggest extracting an agreeable price first and then asking "You, of course, accept major credit cards?" (If you were to ask the credit-card question first the vendor might simply inflate the price to cover his processing fees.) The subtexts of the question are clear: I expect to pay with a credit card and I expect you to accept it since most vendors accept credit cards. Moreover, if I can't pay with a credit card I may not be able to do the deal.

Let's talk for a moment about wording. One of the lessons of this book should be that *how* you ask something is very, very important. Take this credit-card issue. You could certainly ask something like "Could you accept a credit card?" or "Do you accept credit cards?" but this is much weaker trial-balloon type language that implies that this issue is not a deal breaker for you. You are much better off by asking, "You, of course, accept major credit cards?" which is carefully worded and creates the subtexts and desired responses noted above.

When you ask "You, of course, accept major credit cards?" you are putting the seller in a tricky spot. The responses you are likely to get are:

- **Yes.**

- **No.**

- **I prefer a check.**

- **Only up to a certain amount.**

You are, of course, looking for a "yes." You are unlikely to get a "no." Most businesses understand that they need to accept credit cards to survive. Buyers may not have cash on hand or may strongly prefer to use credit cards. A "no" response runs the strong risks of losing your sale. If you do receive a "no" answer you are no worse off than you were before. You can either walk away or agree to another form of payment.

If you are told that the seller "prefers" a check or cash, this is victory. The seller is telegraphing that he will accept the credit card. Tell him that you need to pay with a credit card (since cash is short at the moment) and then move on.

For very large purchases like a car, oftentimes a seller will agree to credit-card payment only up to a certain point. This is fairly common. In this situation if you decide to proceed with the deal you can and should charge up to the maximum amount.

Let's look at a couple of examples.

A few years ago, one of the authors bought a garden shed. Here's about how the negotiation went:

AUTHOR: So you can come down to $3,500 for the shed?

SHED SELLER: Yes.

AUTHOR: That's all-inclusive, delivery, tax, everything?

SHED SELLER: Yes.

AUTHOR: You, of course, accept major credit cards?

SHED SELLER (LONG DELAY): Not usually.

AUTHOR: Cash is short right now. We'd need to pay by Master-Card. If not, we'd have to get back to you when we can raise the cash.

SHED SELLER (LONG DELAY): Okay, we can accept Master-Card from you.

AUTHOR: Great, please e-mail me over a contract to review.

SHED SELLER: Will do.

Notice how we first fixed the best price. This prevented the seller from merely tacking on an extra fee to make up for his credit-card fees. Notice as well how important active listening is in negotiating. We were able to seize upon the hesitation and verbal leak "not usually" in the seller's response. This strongly indicated to the author that the seller was both equipped to take credit cards and was very afraid of losing the sale if he refused to take a credit card. So we pushed. As is usually the case, the seller agreed. The question itself was low risk. If the seller agrees, great. If not, we can always raise the cash quickly and agree to payment by check. Asking "You, of course, accept major credit cards?" earned us $70 in rewards and another month's float on the $3,500 purchase price.

A final quick example. A few years ago, one of the authors bought a small boat. The price was approximately $20,000. Once the favorable price had been agreed upon the author asked, "You, of course, accept major credit cards?" The reply came back that they were accepted for up to $5,000. The author charged the $5,000 and accepted one-fourth of a loaf. Asking the question earned us $100 in rewards. That's $100 for three seconds' worth of question asking. Not a bad result.

Lesson

It is often to your advantage to pay for a purchase via credit card. This is especially true where you are using a credit card that comes with lucrative rewards. To remove any doubt as to whether the seller will accept credit cards you should ask "You, of course, accept major credit cards?" after you have extracted an acceptable price. Under most circumstances the seller will agree to take a credit card for all or part of the payment. The question itself is low risk. If the seller says "no," your options remain open. You can agree to another form of payment or look to another seller.

How to Respond If You Are Asked
"You, of course, accept major credit cards?"

Most of the time the most appropriate answer to this question is a simple "Yes, of course," or, "Yes, up to $5,000." Most businesses understand that they have to bite the bullet and accept credit cards. Not accepting credit cards in this day and age is a risky proposition.

There is also a more aggressive and riskier approach that you can take. This is to state that credit-card payment would result in a higher price. For example, "Yes, but we are then forced to charge a 3 percent convenience fee for doing so."

PART VIII

Deadlock Busters

INTRODUCTION: Deadlock is a common occurrence in negotiations. The questions in this section are designed to help you break deadlock without simply caving in to the other party's demands.

Question #33

WHY DON'T WE JUST SPLIT THE DIFFERENCE?

This simple, direct question is probably the single largest driver of concessions in all of negotiating. The reason for the effectiveness of this question is its apparent appeal to fairness. What could be fairer than both sides making the same concession and splitting the difference? The question seems so fair and reasonable that for many negotiators the urge to say "yes" is almost irresistible. Indeed, the most common response to this question is a simple "sure" or "yes."

Splitting the difference is a technique we've all used in negotiations many times. For example:

PARTY 1: You are asking for $37 per thousand to rent this mailing list bottom line and my final offer is $35 per thousand.

PARTY 2: You have correctly stated the obvious.

PARTY 1: Why don't we split the difference and call it a day?

PARTY 2: Done—and you can call it whatever you want.

For "Can't we just split the difference?" to be most effective, however, it is important to understand the dynamics of how the negotiation is perceived by the superiors (and spouse) of the person you are negotiating with, namely that people want to look like they worked hard to get the best possible deal. The most effective time to deploy this question is after a lengthy negotiation and prolonged impasse. Using the question at this point makes the person you are negotiating with far more likely to report back to their superiors or spouse that he or she did absolutely the best job possible in negotiating and probably couldn't do any better.

Always remember that how the negotiation will be received by superiors is very important to the person you are negotiating with. The recounting of a hard-fought, tough, difficult negotiation will help enhance the stature of the person you are negotiating with in the eyes of his or her superiors or spouse. A quick, down-and-dirty negotiation that reaches the same result can actually be perceived as a failure. Encourage and enable the person you are negotiating with to craft, build, and even embellish his story about how hard your negotiation has been. This is to your benefit and will result in your "Can't we just split the difference?" question having a much better chance of success.

We typically deploy the "Can't we just split the difference?" question after a prolonged period in which the negotiation isn't moving and it seems that an impasse has been reached. This greatly increases the chances of success since it makes you appear to be unwilling to give additional concessions and it allows the person you are negotiating with to demonstrate to superiors that he tried his best to get a better deal. It's also, of course, an effective question because you are softening your demands by 50 percent. By proposing to meet the other party halfway, you allow them to achieve half of their own remaining negotiating goals. Here's how it typically goes for us:

PARTY 1: You say you cannot do the job for less than $50,000?
PARTY 2: Not a penny less.

PARTY 1: I already showed you that my budget is $40,000 and not a penny more.

PARTY 2: I appreciate that, and I called my boss and told her.

PARTY 1: We have not made any progress in a few hours— maybe you should call your boss again and tell her what a hardass I am?

PARTY 2: Good idea, let me paint the picture for her—low expectations always play well back at the home office. I will explain that the deal is hanging by a thread.

PARTY 1: In this case, it's even true. (Said jokingly, but with an undercurrent of truth.)

A brief break occurs while Party 2 calls her boss.

PARTY 2: I called her and I explained that I've sweated through my blue shirt and will be putting it on my expense account, as I don't think it can be salvaged. Plus, I took a second high blood pressure pill.

PARTY 1: Are you being paid enough for this aggravation?

PARTY 2: Absolutely not.

PARTY 1: Why don't we just split the difference?

PARTY 2: We probably should have done that an hour or two ago!

A brief break while Party 2 calls her boss.

PARTY 2 (TO HER EMPLOYER): Hi, it's me again. I might have some good news—I think I can get him up to $45,000. . . . Believe me, this is the absolute most we can get! He has already packed up his laptop. . . . Agreed, I will push him until I get the $45,000. . . . Thank you. I appreciate those kind words.

PARTY 2 (TO PARTY 1): Done at $45,000.

Consider how differently this negotiation might have gone had the split the difference question been used prematurely, before a prolonged deadlock:

PARTY 1: You say you cannot do the job for less than $50,000?

PARTY 2: Not a penny less.

PARTY 1: I already showed you my budget of $40,000 and not a penny more. Why don't we just split the difference?

PARTY 2: Sounds good. Let me call my boss.

PARTY 2 (TO EMPLOYER): Good news. I got him to split the difference and we should take the $45,000. . . . I know that I have only been here forty-five minutes, but I assure you that . . . I have already tried my best and I resent the implication. . . . No, this is not my first negotiation. . . . Okay, I will go back and try to get more. . . .

As you can see, the timing and circumstances under which you ask a question during a negotiation can make all the difference in your results.

Note that if splitting the difference still leaves room to make a profit, albeit even a small one, the recipient is likely to agree. Under some economic conditions people in industries with fixed costs, such as labor, machinery, etc., may even agree to do the deal at a loss to keep the plant running. The key here, of course, is doing research in advance and having the information available, which gets you a good idea of the break-even point of the person you are negotiating with. For example, the invoice price paid by automobile dealers is available on the Internet on various Web sites. Knowing what the dealer needs to get to make a profit can greatly help you decide when the split the difference question will work. So, if you know the dealer's costs are $25,000 and they're offering the car for $26,000 and you state that you won't pay more than $22,000, splitting the difference likely won't work since it would result in a sale price of $24,000 and a $1,000 loss for the dealer. If, on the other hand, you were offering $24,600 and the dealer was asking $25,800, splitting the difference ($25,200) would still put the dealer in profit.

What happens when both sides are at an impasse and each has stated that they have made their best offer? When both sides are entrenched in their respective negotiating positions, the split the difference question can still work. In these cases, a little diplomacy and face-saving may be required. Also, keep in mind that in negotiating, it is common for people to come off their "best and final" positions.

Note that it is absolutely taboo to remind someone that they have come off their "best and final" offer. Rubbing somebody's nose in the dirt is not the way to encourage additional concessions or build goodwill. For example, after you have split the difference you don't want to say to the person you are negotiating with anything like, "I knew you were full of it when you said your previous offer was your last, best, and final one." If you ever have to negotiate with the person again or deal with them in any way, such a comment will likely poison the atmosphere.

Here's how we have typically and successfully handled (with diplomacy and bonding) the situation where both sides have stated they have no further room to negotiate:

> **PARTY 1:** You absolutely can't take less than $50,000 and I absolutely can't offer more than $40,000.
>
> **PARTY 2:** Absolutely correct.
>
> **PARTY 1:** We seem to have both painted ourselves into a corner.
>
> **PARTY 2:** Agreed. Our bosses really haven't given us much room to maneuver here.
>
> **PARTY 1:** Understood. What if we were both to bite the bullet here and we split the difference?
>
> **PARTY 2:** Absolutely—I appreciate your flexibility.
>
> **PARTY 1:** Done. Hey, will you join me for a quick drink to celebrate our agreement?
>
> **PARTY 2:** Absolutely.

A final bit of advice on splitting the difference: By asking this question directly and at the appropriate time during the negotiation, you encourage the person you are negotiating with to make a snap decision, resulting in a 50 percent concession. Experienced negotiators have anticipated this turn of events and intentionally started lower to give themselves plenty of room to make this grand gesture. The key is having an opening position that is credible and serious without being too extreme. Consider how splitting the difference would work out much better for you if your deadlock position was more favorable. Here's the same example as above, but with a different starting position.

> **PARTY 1:** We have been over and over this over and over again. You can't do the job for less than $50,000 and my budget is fixed at $35,000.
> **PARTY 2:** Yes, that is the problem.
> **PARTY 1:** Why don't we just split the difference?
> **PARTY 2:** $42,500 . . . we each take a bit of a hit . . . but at least we have a deal. We share the pain equally. Done.
> **PARTY 1:** Let's call it in to the bosses.

Lesson

"Why don't we just split the difference" can be a very effective way to gain an immediate 50 percent concession from the person you are negotiating with. The question appears inherently reasonable and fair. To maximize the effectiveness of this question, deploy it after a prolonged impasse and negotiate from a position as favorable to yourself as possible.

How to Respond If You Are Asked "Can't we just split the difference?"

In many cases, agreeing to split the difference will result in a reasonable and acceptable outcome to the negotiation. If you feel you should accept the offer and would like to close the deal, your answer will be a simple "yes" or "agreed." Let's say, however, that you can't split the difference (you would either lose money or exceed your authority) or don't believe it is in your best interest to do so. In this scenario, a good response is to explain why you can't split the difference. For example, "I'm sorry, that's my lowest possible pricing." If you wanted to, you could also throw in some power-tool* zingers at the end such as, "I have several other interested parties," or, "Would you like me to recommend someone cheaper?" Alternatively, you can try to put the ball back into the court of the questioner: "I wish I could afford to split the difference and be done with this, but I just can't do it. How much closer can you come to my number? Give me something I can work with and I will make the call to my boss."

* See Part V for more power tools.

Question #34

ARE YOU WILLING TO AGREE TO STAY IN THIS ROOM WITH ME UNTIL WE REACH AN AGREEMENT?

Let's face it, sometimes negotiations get deadlocked. We've all experienced this when negotiating. "Are you willing to agree to stay in this room with me until we reach an agreement?" is a great question to ask when the negotiations are at an impasse.

One of the nice things about this question is how innocent and positive it sounds. Implicit in the question is the fact that you would also like to reach an agreement and that you will probably be willing to make additional concessions.

"Are you willing to agree to stay in this room with me until we reach an agreement?" is highly effective at revealing information. Always keep in mind that when you are negotiating, knowledge is power. The specific types of information revealed by this question often include:

How much the other party wants to reach an agreement. Once the recipient agrees to stay in the room, he has tacitly admitted that he really does want to reach an agreement. Once you know the other party wants an agreement, this puts you in a stronger bargaining position.

How desperate the recipient is to get the deal done. You see, when someone answers "yes" to "Are you willing to agree to stay in this room with me until we reach an agreement?" this strongly tends to indicate that he would prefer to get the deal completed that day. This revelation is very significant because it indicates some level of desperation.

He is willing to make additional concessions. It makes little logical sense for the recipient to agree to stay in the negotiating unless he remains willing to make the additional concessions necessary to reach an agreement.

He either has the authority himself to make additional concessions or can get approval for such concessions quickly. An issue that can come up in negotiations is whether the recipient has authority to make additional concessions. Negotiating with someone who does not have authority is a serious mistake, as there is nothing to be gained since you can make concessions but he cannot. But if he doesn't have to call or e-mail a superior to get additional authority to make concessions, this reveals that he may have the ultimate or unlimited authority to make this deal happen.

The recipient, by agreeing to stay in the room for as long as it takes, will be indicating a high level of investment in getting the deal done. Once you're in a room together, watch for verbal and visual clues indicating that he has reached the point of no return. This revelation is crucial, if you can pick it up, because it gives you tremendous negotiating power and leverage. Once you have determined that the recipient really can't leave without a deal you are in a position to push very hard for major concessions to, as they say, "get the deal done today."

Keep in mind that it is often best to grant a minor concession (even if you do not have to) so the recipient can save face and justify all the concessions he makes to his superiors. Also keep in mind that it's often easier to win more of your own points when you concede a few minor ones to the person you are negotiating with. Of course, always remember that when you're in that room you don't want to appear desperate for a deal or you will be the one losing the bargaining power.

Note that when the recipient of the question answers "no," any one of the following factors may be the reason:

He does not have the authority to make the concessions necessary to stay until an agreement is reached. In this case you are best advised to suspend the negotiation until someone with authority to make concessions is available to negotiate with you.

He does not want to appear to be too eager to reach an agreement, thereby weakening his negotiation stance. You can easily counter this by calling his bluff and stating, "Okay, thank you for your time. I'll pursue other options instead."

He may not have the time to stay. If this is the case, you may consider responding, "When will you be available?" His response to this follow-up question will further measure his level of interest in making a deal happen.

The recipient may feel that the parties are too far apart to reach an agreement. This is good to know, too, as it will save your wasting further time trying to pursue a deal.

It's your responsibility to follow up and determine why the recipient will not agree to stay in the room.

Consider this example from our own experiences where we used "Are you willing to agree to stay in this room with me until we reach an agreement?" to turn a disastrous and confrontational negotiation into a win-win. Many years ago, we had another partner in business with us. Things didn't work out and he wanted to sell his interest in the business. Because of legal restrictions the only person he could really sell out to was us.

He was in particular need of money at the time and things quickly deteriorated. He hired a lawyer and threatened to sue us. We received numerous nasty letters from his attorney. The situation looked like it was headed to a no-win situation with lawsuits and wasted time where only the lawyers would make money.

We happened to see our ex-partner at a meeting we were all attending. Upon seeing him I asked, "Are you willing to agree to stay together here with me until we reach an agreement?" He said "yes" and there was an immediate release of tension. We went to a quiet room and discussed things one-on-one with no lawyers involved. After about an hour we reached an agreement. I agreed to pay a little more than I had previously offered to buy him out. He was happy. The premium I had paid was well worth resolving the situation and avoiding the cost and distraction of lawsuits. He was happy because he got more money for his shares. We were both happy because we were able to reconcile and we remain friends to this day. My asking the question "Are you willing to agree to stay in this room with me until we reach an agreement?" allowed all of this to happen.

Another example is the Good Friday Peace Agreement. When Senator George Mitchell was negotiating the Good Friday Agreement in Ireland, a deadline of April 9, the day before Good Friday, was set. The parties negotiated for thirty hours without sleep. Finally, the designated hour passed without an agreement. The parties agreed to unplug the clock and stay in the room until they reached an agreement. A negotiated agreement was achieved. Agreeing to reach an agreement saved countless lives and improved the lives of countless more.

One final example. Remember that all negotiations are not zero-sum adversarial ones. Many times, colleagues, spouses, and others cannot agree on a course of action and spend countless hours going back and forth on what to do. This happens in our business all the time. Often, the partners are at odds as to what to do and cannot reach a consensus. This can paralyze the company. When faced with such potentially damaging paralysis, we often all agree to lock ourselves into a room until we reach a consensus and can move on.

Lesson

When faced with a deadlock, consider asking the question "Are you willing to agree to stay in this room with me until we reach an agreement?" This question can and has been used to effectively determine if a deadlock can be broken, gain valuable information, help save you from wasting time in negotiations that are likely to be fruitless, and push things to a conclusion.

How to Respond If You Are Asked "Are you willing to agree to stay in this room with me until we reach an agreement?"

The key to most effectively answering this question is to do so in a manner that projects negotiating power. An unqualified "yes" should be avoided as such an answer may make you appear desperate for a deal and this would weaken your negotiating position.

Ways to answer this question that project power include, "I can talk a little bit more, but I have other interested parties, so my time is limited," or, "If you commit to being flexible we can agree to continue our discussions." Alternatively, a reply such as "Why do you think this would help?" will force the questioner to explain and justify, and will likely reveal useful information.

Question #35

SHOULD I CLOSE MY FILE?

One of the most frustrating things in business is people not getting back to you. There are many reasons for this, including that they may be busy, distracted, not interested in dealing with you, or just plain lazy. The authors have had tremendous success with the question "Should I close my file?" It is a superb way to deal with a person you are negotiating with who:

- is nonresponsive;

- has been dragging his heels;

- is evasive;

- has been unable to make a decision; or

- is unduly delaying reaching some kind of agreement.

We have found that this question is best delivered in writing via e-mail or snail mail. There are many reasons for this. First, the procrastinator you are dealing with probably doesn't pick up his phone or return phone calls. Second, putting the question in writing may create additional anxiety in the recipient from the fact that there is now a written record, which shows evidence that he may have dropped the ball.

The question itself is well designed in that it is a very polite way of pushing a procrastinator to action. You are not threatening, yelling, or angry; you are just asking if you should close your file. Another advantage implicit in the question is the fact that you are not overeager for a deal, which helps you to build negotiating power. One final advantage is that when you do hear back, you often receive a quick off-the-cuff reply that contains valuable information and strengthens your bargaining position.

We have found the question "Should I close my file?" to be equally effective whether you are the buyer or seller in a negotiation when you have repeatedly not heard back from the person you are negotiating with. In all cases, we recommend that the question be delivered with a very light touch and that it allow the person you are negotiating with to save face.

We have used "Should I close my file?" innumerable times in our own dealings. We have found more than 50 percent of the time it is effective in moving a stalled negotiation forward.

A common time we use this question is when we are selling our consulting services. In many instances, we are contacted by a prospective client and then prepare and deliver a detailed proposal, including a price for the consulting or training services that they have requested. Oftentimes, we receive no further response so we follow up via e-mail or voice mail. After three to four attempts, we deploy the "Should I close my file?" question. Here's how it typically goes.

E-mail sent to procrastinator:

Dear Fred,
I have been unable to reach you via e-mail and phone.
Should I close my file?
Regards,
Steve

The authors have used this simple five-word question many times with excellent results. These results usually appear immediately, on the same business day the question was asked. More often than not, we'll get back a written response or voice mail something like this:

Steve:
Please do not close your file. I have been overwhelmed with work here. What is the best time to talk or meet? We really need your help—it's hitting the fan here.
Thank you for your patience,
Fred

Note how Fred also stated that they really needed our help. This type of helpful information leak is very common in the responses you will receive to the "Should I close my file?" question.

We have also used this question effectively when we are the potential buyers. Here's what typically happens when we are unable to come to terms with a seller and are deadlocked. Before ending the deadlocked conversation, we ask the person we are negotiating with to go back and study the situation and see if they can come up with a better figure. A few days after this, when we haven't heard from them, we'll send an e-mail along the lines of the following:

Dear Susan:
Thank you very much for discussing the possibility of our entering into a long-term relationship with you.

I haven't received a revised proposal from you.
Should I close my file?
Thank you for all your help,
Jim

Notice how we asked politely and dangled the possibility of a long-term relationship in front of them. The response we most often get to this is something like:

Dear Jim:
Don't close that file! I talked to our team here and we're able to come down to your number. I tried to call you just now. I will try you again in a bit.
I look forward to doing business with you.
Regards,
Susan

Lesson

The "Should I close my file?" question is extraordinarily effective in getting attention, action, apologies, and an excellent negotiated agreement. It is best asked in writing and in a polite, nonthreatening manner that allows the person you are negotiating with to save face.

How to Respond If You Are Asked "Should I close my file?"

As seen above, the one thing to avoid when responding to this question is any information that weakens your bargaining position. Specifically, avoid any statement begging the person to keep their file open or suggesting that you really need their help.

Depending upon the situation, you may be able to respond in a way that actually strengthens your bargaining position. The idea is to slip into your response information that makes it appear that you are not in a rush and/or have alternatives. For example: "Ted, thanks for your note. When you wouldn't move on your price we figured you weren't interested, so we are close to finalizing with another vendor. If you would like to be considered, please send over a revised proposal ASAP. Regards, Jim."

Question #36

DOES [THE PERSON YOU ARE NEGOTIATING WITH] STILL WORK THERE?

It takes two to tango when it comes to negotiating. The person you are negotiating with has to be responsive in order for you to reach a successful agreement in a reasonable amount of time. Unfortunately, all too often the person you are negotiating with is nonresponsive. "Does [the person you are negotiating with] still work there?" is designed to deal with a nonresponsive negotiating partner.

A nonresponsive negotiating partner can create havoc for your schedule for completing a negotiation. If you are gathering competing bids, a nonresponsive bidder can limit your options and negotiating leverage. If you are under a time crunch to get your negotiation done, an unnecessary delay can cost you large amounts of money. The situation of being in a time crunch can be a particularly dicey one in that you do not want the other side to know or suspect that you are in a time crunch. Asking the supervisor of the person you are negotiating with "Does [the person you are negotiating with] still work there?" can be wildly effective in immediately transforming a nonresponsive negotiating partner into a very responsive one.

The subtext of "Does [the person you are negotiating with] still work there?" is clear. By asking the supervisor of the person you are negotiating with this question, you are suggesting that the person has been so neglectful of their responsibilities and so unresponsive that you are assuming they must have left the company. The underlying message is so powerful that the results of asking this question are usually immediate and dramatic.

"Does [the person you are negotiating with] still work there?" is not to be used lightly, prematurely, or in bad faith. In order for this question to be effective it must be based on credible facts. A prerequisite for use is a strong pattern of unresponsiveness. We suggest a minimum of three unreturned phone calls or e-mails over a period of two to three days. If this question is deployed prematurely you run the risks of losing credibility, looking like a troublemaker, angering the person you were negotiating with, and looking like a lunatic. "Does [the person you are negotiating with] still work there?" is in effect a last-resort question designed to dramatically increase the pace of negotiations and to gain additional concessions.

When using "Does [the person you are negotiating with] still work there?" you should make sure that you never imply that you are desperate for a deal. If you appear desperate you will lose negotiating power and the question could very well backfire on you. Not appearing to need a deal can require a delicate balancing act. One way not to appear desperate is to include information that suggests along with the question that you are bidding out possibilities and was surprised that the company you are negotiating with didn't want to be considered. By using this technique you send the message that you have several other alternatives.

All hell is likely to break loose on the other side after this question has been asked. There is nothing more frustrating to a supervisor than a subordinate who is lazy, procrastinating, and not doing his job. It's one thing to lose a deal because of circumstances outside of your control. To lose a deal because of the nonfeasance of an employee can be absolutely infuriating. We have found "Does [the person you are negotiating with] still work there?" to be incredibly effective at immediately and dramatically increasing the responsiveness from the other side. Because of the inherent risk of the question and because it can have adverse professional consequences on the person we are negotiating with, we use this question only as a last resort and only when time is of the essence.

"Does [the person you are negotiating with] still work there?" is often doubly effective. When a supervisor receives this question he is likely to immediately get in touch with the person you had been negotiating with and find out what the story is. If that person has indeed dropped the ball, he will be sternly reprimanded for potentially costing the organization a deal. After such a reprimand the person you are negotiating with really, really doesn't want to lose the deal. We have found that after this question is used the person you are negotiating with is more responsive and also far more accommodating in terms of the negotiation itself.

The other likely response to "Does [the person you are negotiating with] still work there?" is that the supervisor will apologize and inform you that they are taking over the matter personally. This is also a very good result for you. You are generally best off negotiating with a person as high in the chain of command as possible. In addition, this supervisor will know that you are now going to be a tough sell that needs to be won over and will usually be very accommodating to you.

We have found that the best way to use this question is in written form. Sending an e-mail (fax or letter in days past) allows you to put context to your story by throwing in other facts such as what you have done to contact the person and what you now plan on doing in terms of the deal. Let's look at a couple of examples.

In a former life, one of the authors was a particularly aggressive personal injury lawyer. I was representing a gentleman who suffered an amputation of his right leg at the knee after an accident. There was no question that the other party was legally responsible for the accident.

I contacted the adjuster who was assigned to settle the case. He did not respond. I called a second and third time. No reply whatsoever. I followed up with letters, faxes and more phone calls. He would not reply. After getting more than a little frustrated at the lack of responsiveness I had six color photographs taken of what was left of my client's leg (oozing pus and all) and sent them to the president of the billion-dollar insurance company with this cover letter:

> I am representing Mr. Brown. As you can see from the enclosed photographs he suffered a severe injury. There are no issues about who is responsible for the accident. I have tried repeatedly to have Mr. Jones, the adjuster assigned to the case, return my phone calls, letters, and faxes (see enclosed) to no avail.
>
> I have only one question:
> Does Mr. Jones still work for you?
> Thank you for your help
> P.S. I am sure that your company normally operates in good faith to resolve these uncontested cases.

Shortly after the letter went out I received a phone call from the president of this large insurance company. Here is how it went:

> I received your letter and can assure you of several things:

1. *Mr. Jones does still work for us.*

2. *He will be calling you immediately.*

3. *We will continue to operate in good faith.*

> Thank you for calling this matter to my attention. Oh, by the way, please do not send any more graphic color photos

like that to my office. My administrative assistant who
handles my mail was not a combat surgeon and is not used
to these kinds of photos.

Within five days the adjuster, who apparently had been read
the riot act, called me, apologized for the "misunderstanding," and
resolved the case with me on a very favorable basis to my client.

More recently, we were conducting some contractual negotiations
with a hotel to bring one of our meetings to a particular venue. The
deal with the hotel was worth well over $100,000 in revenue to the
hotel. For various business reasons we needed to resolve the negotiations quickly but we obviously didn't want the hotel to know
that. We received a draft contract, marked it up, and sent it back to
our contact. Nothing. We called, left a message, and asked that the
revised contract be sent back. No response. We sent a follow-up
e-mail asking for a revised contract. Nothing. We called the contact and got voice mail. We pressed ZERO for immediate assistance
and the message said the line was no longer in service. We liked
our contact very much and didn't want to get him in trouble, but
we finally had no choice and sent an e-mail to his supervisor.

> *Dear Mr. Smith:*
> *Does Mr. Jones still work at your hotel? We have tried*
> *repeatedly to finalize a large sales contract with him but*
> *have not heard back from him. We hope very much that*
> *everything is okay. Please let us know if you'd still like to be*
> *considered for this contract or if you will not be bidding for*
> *our business.*

The results were immediate and impressive. Within twenty minutes we received a phone call from the supervisor we had sent the
e-mail to. He was extremely apologetic. He told us that they were

short staffed and that our contact had been doing the job of three people. He also told us that we would have our contract changes within the hour. We did. Not only did we get an answer, but we were given everything that we had asked for. We were able to finalize the contract on very favorable terms within two hours of the e-mail to the supervisor going out. What's more, ever since that e-mail went out we have received extremely responsive service from everyone at the hotel, including our original contact who had been nonresponsive.

Lesson

Asking the supervisor of a nonresponsive negotiating partner "Does [the person you are negotiating with] still work there?" can be extremely effective at both dramatically increasing responsiveness and gaining concessions. This question should be used only as a last resort after the person you are negotiating with has been repeatedly nonresponsive. If you use this question in inappropriate circumstances it will likely backfire on you. The question is best asked in writing. When asking this question you should be very careful to not appear to be desperate for a deal. If you do appear desperate, the question will backfire on you. This question is not for the faint of heart as it can have significant negative professional consequences on the person you were negotiating with.

How to Respond If You Are Asked "Does [the person you are negotiating with] still work there?"

This is not a question you want to receive. If you do receive it, it either means that the person you are negotiating with is a jerk, your employee dropped the ball, or something else went wrong such as faulty e-mail communications. How you respond to this question will, of course, depend upon the situation.

If you determine that this question was sent unfairly or in bad faith, you should ask yourself if you really want to deal with the person who sent it. In this situation, a good response might be to politely refer the person to a competitor that you do not like. For example, "Thank you for your note. We have looked into things and determined that we will be unable to meet your needs. I suggest you contact John Smith at 555-555-4567 as he may be able to help you. Thank you again for your inquiry."

If you determine that an employee hasn't been responsive, you need to find out why. If there is a legitimate reason that will help your bargaining position, don't be afraid to use it. For example, "Mr. Angelo, thank you for your note. We are sorry that Ms. Tarlow hasn't been able to get back to you. Things have been crazy here with inquiries and sales, and she has needed to prioritize with the best prospects. Your offering prices were such that she felt you were not a serious inquiry. If you have flexibility on your offer, please feel free to contact either Ms. Tarlow or me. Thank you again for your inquiry."

If the nonresponsiveness was a result of a legitimate emergency you can consider stating so. For example, "I am very sorry that Ms. Tarlow hasn't been able to get back to you. She had a death in the family. I will call you shortly to discuss your needs."

You can also give as a response a legitimate reason for not getting their messages. For example, "I am sorry for this. We looked into it and for whatever reason your e-mails had been going into Ms. Tarlow's spam folder. She'll get back to you immediately. Thank you again."

Where you have no excuses and it is clear that your employee dropped the ball you should take charge of the situation yourself.* In your response you should not provide any information that will weaken your bargaining position or inflame the other person. Take over the negotiation and don't get into any specifics about the past— move the focus onto the deal. For example, "Mr. Angelo. I am very sorry nobody got back to you. I will handle your account personally. When is a good time to call you today?"

---

* You'll also want to remember to deal with the nonresponsive employee.

Question #37

ARE YOU WILLING TO GET CREATIVE HERE TO TRY TO FIND SOMETHING THAT WORKS FOR BOTH OF US?

"Are you willing to get creative here to find something that works for both of us?" is a situational question. The specific situation it is designed to handle is deadlock. It is properly used where you believe the other party is negotiating in good faith and is looking for a win-win solution.

"Are you willing to get creative here to find something that works for both of us?" can be very effective at breaking a deadlock. When the parties are deadlocked, they both may need to take a step back, think outside the box, and consider new approaches. This question will help reenergize the participants to the negotiation and encourage them to look for new and innovative win-win solutions.

The subtexts of the question are simple: What's on the table doesn't work for me. Let's find something that works for both of us. If you agree to be creative, so will I. "Are you willing to get creative here to find something that works for both of us?" is designed to, in essence, solicit an agreement by which both parties agree to consider modifying their positions, making concessions, varying demands or terms, etc. An affirmative reply by the person you are negotiating with can be a significant concession in and of itself. This is because while the person you are negotiating with has not agreed on any specific concessions, his agreeing to get creative is an acknowledgement that the current proposal doesn't work for you and is a tacit agreement to consider additional concessions.

The question is effective because it is so difficult to resist. What can be more reasonable than to ask for the other person to tap into their creativity to help find a solution that benefits both parties? Refusal to agree would likely be seen as a lack of cooperation and a lack of good faith. Also, what does the person you are negotiating with have to lose by agreeing to get creative?

"Are you willing to get creative here to find something that works for both of us?" has the added benefit of gently reminding the person you are negotiating with that what is on the table presently does not work for you. As such, you might be forced to walk away. If that happens, the person you are negotiating with will lose the deal.

Once you get the person you are negotiating with to answer yes to this question, it is best practice to follow up with a question such as "Do you have any ideas?" or "How else might we be able to find a solution here?" or "Why don't you think about it and see what you can come up with?" The idea is to encourage the person you are negotiating with to make a proposal. If you are fortunate, this proposal may contain a very valuable concession for you.

If the person you are negotiating with will not put forth a creative solution, you will need to consider proposing one yourself. This obviously needs to be done with caution. You do not want to hastily make a proposal that hasn't been thoroughly thought out. You also want to be careful that you do not negotiate against yourself. That is, if your new idea contains a concession, you'll also want to be asking for concessions from the other party.

"Are you willing to get creative here to find something that works for both of us?" is a well-designed question because either a positive or negative reply will help your negotiation. If the question is resisted, this can be a big red flag that the person you are negotiating with is not looking for a win-win solution and is not likely to make any meaningful concessions. When that happens, you should seriously consider walking away from the negotiation and exploring other alternatives.

We've used this example to great effect over the years where we've been deadlocked but it seemed that we should be able to reach a win-win solution. For example, recently we were looking to get some custom software developed for us. We were far apart on price with the programmer, and the negotiation had become deadlocked. Using "Are you willing to get creative here to find something that works for both of us?" allowed us to come up with the creative solution of a lowered price in exchange for a relaxed time deadline. Here's about how the negotiation went:

> **AUTHORS:** We would like you to do some programming for us on some software we are developing. I sent you the specs. What are we looking at in terms of cost?
>
> **PROGRAMMER:** This is not as simple as it would look.
>
> **AUTHORS:** It never is.
>
> **PROGRAMMER:** I will just let that slide. You are looking at $25,000 if you do not make any changes to the specs and the scope of the project.
>
> **AUTHORS:** I'm sure you are worth it, but that is way out of our price range.
>
> **PROGRAMMER:** What is your budget?
>
> **AUTHORS:** We have budgeted $7,500.
>
> **PROGRAMMER:** You are not even close.
>
> **AUTHORS:** Are you willing to get creative to make this work?
>
> **PROGRAMMER:** What do you have in mind?
>
> **AUTHORS:** How soon can you get this to us?
>
> **PROGRAMMER:** I am tied up for months with customers who actually have money and are willing to part with it. Maybe three months if we can agree on price.

AUTHORS: What if we let you develop this as fill-in work—no time deadlines?

PROGRAMMER: That would make it more attractive.

AUTHORS: How about $10,000, no time constraints, and a $7,500 deposit?

PROGRAMMER: Done. Just don't call me in two weeks asking if it's finished yet.

Here's another example. We negotiate with a lot of hotels where we hold the seminars and conferences that our company puts on. A common sticking point in these negotiations is that the hotel often insists that we agree to be financially responsible for all the hotel rooms that the hotel is putting on hold for use by our attendees. This is called an "attrition clause" in the meeting industry and it's a very big deal. The problem is that if we have a poor attendance, attrition can be financially ruinous for us since we have to pay for all the unused hotel rooms that were held for our attendees. We never agree to attrition and as such negotiations often deadlock on this point. Here's how we broke such a deadlock a few years ago.

HOTEL: It looks like we've agreed on everything except the attrition.

AUTHORS: Yes, as we've explained, that's a line-in-the-sand issue for us. We love your hotel. We'd like to make this a regular location for our conferences.

HOTEL: We understand, but we need to be protected, too.

AUTHORS: Are you willing to get creative here to try to find something that works for both of us?

HOTEL: Of course. You know that we want your business.

AUTHORS: Why don't you brainstorm with your team and see what you can come up with?

Notice how we asked them to come up with a creative idea (i.e., a concession). A few hours later we got a call. What if the hotel agreed to waive the attrition clause, but in return, they would closely modify how many of our sleeping rooms were actually being reserved by attendees? If things looked like they were going slowly, they would reserve the right to reduce the number of rooms they were holding for us and resell these rooms to the public. This worked for us so we readily agreed, and we've been doing mutually profitable business with them for many years since. "Are you willing to get creative here to find something that works for both of us?" broke a potential deadlock and led directly to a win-win solution.

Lesson

"Are you willing to get creative here to find something that works for both of us?" can be very effective in helping to break a deadlock. The question is low risk and difficult to resist. If the person you are negotiating with agrees, try to encourage them to come up with the creative solution. If the person you are negotiating with won't even agree to try to get creative, it's probably time to consider your alternatives and walk away from the negotiation.

How to Respond If You Are Asked "Are you willing to get creative here to find something that works for both of us?"

The way to respond to this question is to be open but also to put the onus on the other person to come up with the solution, since this would need to contain a concession. You generally do not want to come up with the solution because this may tip your hand as to what you may be willing to give up. For example, "Of course. What do you have in mind?" If you are pressed to come up with the creative solution the question can be easily handled with a simple "I'll need to think about that. If I can come up with something, I'll let you know."

Question #38

WOULD YOU LIKE TO GO OFF THE RECORD HERE?

This is another great question to use when a negotiation gets deadlocked. When a deadlock arises, the formality of your negotiating session may be one of the problems. What often occurs is that each side is afraid to offer concessions without getting anything back in return. "Would you like to go off the record here?" is designed to move negotiations along when the parties are bogged down defending their respective positions.

A frank, off-the-record discussion frequently produces significant progress due to the fact that:

- It immediately relaxes the atmosphere.

- The parties are not officially offering or accepting anything.

- Off-the-record discussions enable the parties to soften their entrenched positions.

- An off-the-record format encourages trial balloons: e.g., "If I was able to get $125,000 would you accept it?"

- The parties are able to call superiors in their respective companies to tentatively get authority to make concessions.

- It encourages an "us against them"/"we are both in the same boat" mentality where the negotiators can bond by sharing their common burden of trying to please demanding superiors. Once both parties recognize or accept the fact that their superiors may have given them unrealistic marching orders, they may be better positioned to work together to problem solve.

It has been our experience when using this question that the reply is almost always "yes" or "okay." After you receive a "yes" response, a good symbolic way of demonstrating that you are now off the record is to put down your pen, put away your notepad, or close your laptop lid. Once you are off the record, try to build a personal bond with the person you are negotiating with. Then you can proceed to float some trial balloons or get across a message that you feel would empower you. Let's take a look how this technique has worked for us.

We were lawyers in our former lives. As attorneys we had numerous opportunities to negotiate hundreds of cases to settlement. The question "Would you like to go off the record?" was very helpful in breaking impasses in the negotiating process. Here is an example of a telephone negotiation.

ATTORNEY: Your position is that the maximum you can pay in this case is $50,000?

ADJUSTER: Absolutely. That is all that I can pay and not a penny more.

ATTORNEY: My client has instructed me not to accept a penny less than $100,000.

ADJUSTER: Understood. Where do we go from here?

ATTORNEY: Would you be willing to go off the record here?

ADJUSTER: What have we got to lose?

ATTORNEY: Put your pen down, and I am putting my pen down as well. What are we going to do with my unreasonable client and your ridiculous manager? How do they expect you to settle these cases if they don't give you enough money?

ADJUSTER: You don't know the half of it. Come over one day and see our GOYA chart.

ATTORNEY: GOYA?

ADJUSTER: Yes, a big chart that hangs on the wall here—it has all the cases and how many each adjuster has left to resolve. We call it the GOYA chart—the Get Off Your Ass chart!

ATTORNEY: How nice. If I could get my client to move off the $100,000 could you get the manager to get off *his* ass?

ADJUSTER: They just dropped eleven more cases on my desk. Could you take $75,000?

ATTORNEY: No, but I will push him to the wall with $80,000.

ADJUSTER: I will go see the manager. Don't disappoint me.

Notice how the attorney above was able to get the adjuster to believe that the attorney was on his side against the adjuster's superiors. Off-the-record remarks facilitate this.

We've also used the off-the-record technique in a real estate transaction when dealing with a seller's agent:

AUTHOR: Okay, it seems as though we're $25,000 apart on price.

SELLER'S AGENT: Yeah, the sellers aren't inclined to come down any more.

AUTHOR: Can we go off the record?

SELLER'S AGENT: Sure, why not.

AUTHOR: Look, I don't even want to move. I like the house we are in now just fine. This is all my spouse's idea. Are you married?

SELLER'S AGENT: Been there, done that. I see where you're coming from. I'll let them know you're not coming up any higher.

In this example, the seller's price came down and met the buyer's price. The agent went back and leaked the "confidential" information that the buyers weren't motivated and the seller caved on the price. The off-the-record question was skillfully used to bond with the agent and deliver a power-building message—that the buyers weren't motivated—in a credible way. Note also the verbal leak "aren't inclined" by the agent. Active listening skills are crucial for good negotiations to develop.

Lesson

Asking to go off the record can be a very effective negotiating question when faced with deadlock. It breaks the tension, allows bonding, and facilitates trial balloons.

How to Respond If You Are Asked "Would you like to go off the record here?"

There are a couple of different ways you might want to respond to this question. The most obvious is simply to say "yes" and hear out what the other person has to say. If the other party is not a good negotiator, the information might actually be helpful to you.

If the person you are dealing with is a superior negotiator, it is likely that the off-the-record comment will be calculated somehow to weaken you or is part of a gambit. In this situation you might want to politely say "no." There are different ways to do this. For example, you could say in a good spirited way, "One thing my lawyer always tells me is that there is no such thing as off the record." You might also respond with something like "One rule I follow is that I don't want to know any secrets. It makes life much simpler. So please, if you want something kept confidential, I don't want to know. I hope you understand." Alternatively, you could politely decline by saying, "My corporate ethical policy does not permit off-the-record conversations."

Question #39

CAN YOU RECOMMEND SOMEONE ELSE?

"Can you recommend someone else?" is a question for buyers. It is an immensely potent question and can instantly and dramatically increase your bargaining position. The subtexts of the question are clear and powerful: I need something. You are not providing it. I am not happy. I have all the power in this situation and am actively mapping out my options for walking away from you.

Like many excellent negotiating questions, "Can you recommend someone else?" is, on its face, polite and low key, but it puts the seller you are negotiating with in a very difficult position. You are quite clearly delivering a stark wake-up call to the seller that you are within a hair of saying sayonara to them. When this message hits home (and it will almost instantly), the seller will be in the position of either giving ground or losing you as a customer. Business and human nature being what they are, if a seller can give ground after hearing this question, he usually will.

"Can you recommend someone else?" does carry a good deal of inherent risk if it is used as a bluff. If you are being unreasonable in your demands and attitude, a frustrated seller may gladly refer you to a competitor that he doesn't like. If that happens, you may be out of luck if you really wanted to deal with the seller you asked the question of. If you stay with the seller you asked the question of, your bluff will be called and you will have lost a good deal of negotiating leverage. We recommend that you do not use "Can you recommend someone else?" as a bluff unless you are well prepared to risk a worse bargaining position with the seller you are dealing with.

The ideal time to unleash "Can you recommend someone else?" is when the seller has taken an unreasonable and firm position that simply does not work for you. In this situation, "Can you recommend someone else?" carries no risk because you have nothing to lose—the seller isn't indicating that they can or will give you what you need.

We have found that this question can pretty much work magic in turning around a previously inflexible seller. "Can you recommend someone else?" will often work out to be the final clincher question, which quickly and decisively gets you what you had been asking for. We often use this question to great effect when we have reached deadlock with a seller and are ready, willing, and able to walk away.

"Can you recommend someone else?" can be particularly effective against sellers that you have a long-term relationship with. The threat of walking away has its greatest efficacy in regards to long-term sellers as these have the most to lose. Such sellers often get complacent and take your business for granted. When complacency develops, the level of service you receive can suffer dramatically. The implicit threat of walking away contained in "Can you recommend someone else?" can often instantly get you what you want and need. Let's look at a couple of examples.

Our business needs a lot of printing. We recently ran into a pretty big problem with one printer that we regularly use. "Can you recommend someone else?" solved our problem.

First, some background. We had been using a particular printer for a number of years. We gave this printer around $30,000 to $50,000 worth of business each year. We got pretty good service, which gradually deteriorated over time. Very recently, we needed to get some printing done on an emergency basis. We stood to lose $20,000 to $30,000 in lost profits if we couldn't get this simple little printing job taken care of.

We called for a quote. No response. We called a second and third time, and explained the urgency of the situation. Finally, we got a call back from the customer service person we had been dealing with. She explained that this was "impossible" as they were very busy, she had other customers to deal with, and that they might be able to get us the job we were asking for in a couple of weeks. Unfortunately, as they well knew, we *needed* the job delivered to us in two days. We suspected strongly that the customer service person we were dealing with was a little lazy and simply wasn't overly eager to juggle her schedule and do extra work on her end to help us out. What was in it for her but more work?

At this point we had nothing to lose. We needed the job in two days. If they didn't want our business, we'd have to find somebody that did. The customer-service person was obviously a dead end. We called the owner of the printing company and explained what we needed and how we were surprised that they couldn't accommodate us. (You would think that a printer would be able to print something.) It was a very short conversation. We asked one question and with a deadly serious tone: "Congratulations on your being so busy that you can turn away business. We love a success story. All we're looking for is a printer who is able to print and values our business. We realize that we're a small account that's only worth $300,000 to $500,000 over ten years. You've been in the field many years. Can you recommend someone else?" Asking the question was like waving a magic wand. We instantly received apologies, a statement of appreciation for our business, and assurances that they could and would get the job we needed done for us in the time frame we needed. We can only imagine the conversation that later went down between the owner and the customer-service rep we had been dealing with.

The reasons we were able to get what we wanted were that we talked to the right person* and asked the right question. The right person was the owner. The owner had much to lose by not acceding to our request. The customer-service rep's incentives were perverse. She would have to do more work if she helped us and that is something she apparently wasn't overly eager to do.

The right question was "Can you recommend someone else?" This indicated that we were ready and willing to walk away. We clearly laid out in advance of this question that we were asking for a reasonable thing (printing from a printer). We also helped make this question work by suggesting that the owner had $300,000 to $500,000 to lose if we walked away. As often is the case, "Can you recommend someone else?" immediately resulted in our getting 100 percent of what we were looking for.

Here's a second example. Recently, one of the authors needed some work done by a local contractor that he had been doing regular business with for a couple of years. The work needed to be done within a few weeks but wasn't an emergency. I called up the contractor's office and got his assistant. I explained what I needed done. The conversation with his assistant was almost surreal and close to comical. Apparently, we had run into somebody without the authority, initiative, or common sense to be in any way flexible. Here's about how the conversation went:

> **AUTHOR:** When can you come out?
> **CONTRACTOR'S ASSISTANT:** Tomorrow between 8 A.M. and noon.

---

* For more on the importance of dealing with the right person, please see Part II.

AUTHOR: Well, I have something very important that I have to do between 9 and 10, which can't be moved. Can you do another day?

CONTRACTOR'S ASSISTANT: No.

AUTHOR: Okay, can you just make sure that you come after 10 tomorrow? Then we can do it tomorrow.

CONTRACTOR'S ASSISTANT: No, we don't work that way.

AUTHOR: Okay, let's just schedule another day.

CONTRACTOR'S ASSISTANT: I'm sorry. Tomorrow's the day we are planning on being in your area.

AUTHOR: Are you telling me that tomorrow between 8 and 12 is the only time between now and the end of eternity that you can come out and do the work?

CONTRACTOR'S ASSISTANT: That's when we'll be in your area.

AUTHOR: Can you ask the owner to give me a call? Here's my cell number.

CONTRACTOR'S ASSISTANT: I will ask him.

That evening the owner called. I explained the remarkable conversation that I had had with his assistant, apologized for bothering him, and then asked, "Can you recommend someone else that might be willing to come out here for this?" The reply was immediate. "No need. I'll have someone there at 8:00 A.M. on Thursday if that works for you." It did, and he showed up right on time. By talking to the right person—the owner—and asking the right question, we were able to get our very reasonable request for service acceded to.

Lesson

If you are willing to walk away from a seller consider asking them, "Can you recommend someone else?" This question will be most effective when you have reached deadlock and are indeed willing to walk away. It can be particularly effective if used on a seller with whom you have a long-term relationship as these sellers have the most to lose if you walk. "Can you recommend someone else?" is best directed to someone in a position of authority at the seller. This question is risky if used as a bluff since the seller may, in fact, call your bluff—especially if what you were asking for was unreasonable or you're difficult to deal with.

How to Respond If You Are Asked "Can you recommend someone else?"

The best response to this question depends upon your bargaining leverage, your goals, and how much risk you want to take. If you feel you are in a strong bargaining position and you have good alternatives, an effective response is to call the other party's bluff. For example, "Sure, do you have a pen? There are many down-and-dirty providers that will probably be cheaper and aren't as busy as us."

If, on the other hand, you do have room to negotiate, don't believe the other person is bluffing, and don't want to risk losing the deal, a good response is to get the focus back on the negotiation. For example, "I don't think that will be necessary, I'm sure we can work something out" or, "Well, we can certainly come out there tomorrow if you need us to. No problem." Always keep in mind that if the person asking the question is a long-term valuable client you will usually want to be extra careful not to lose the account. Longtime customers are very valuable and can be very difficult to replace.

Question #40

WHAT CAN YOU GIVE ME THAT I CAN TAKE BACK TO MY BOSS?

The purpose of negotiating is to obtain concessions. "What can you give me that I can take back to my boss?" is a simple question that can be very effective at encouraging concessions from the person you are negotiating with. The subtexts of the question are fairly simple: My boss is the ultimate decision maker, I need to look good in front of my boss, he's not happy now, and I need a sweetener to make this deal close.

There are many advantages to utilizing the boss for your hard negotiating position. First, by pointing to what your boss needs you are communicating that you don't just *want* more concessions, you *need* them. If the party you are negotiating with believes that you need concessions in order to complete a deal, he will also realize that failure to grant them will likely result in a blown deal and a blown opportunity.

A second advantage of "What can you give me that I can take back to my boss?" is that it can help the negotiating parties bond. Everybody has or has had a boss. By pointing out that you are at the mercy of your boss you are making yourself more sympathetic to the person you are negotiating with, since they've been or may be in the same position themselves. If that person has sympathy for you and likes you, he will be more likely to grant you concessions. In addition, the fact that your boss, not you, is to blame for your demands will help minimize any animosity or hard feelings that could get in the way of the negotiation process.

A third advantage of "What can you give me that I can take back to my boss?" is that it puts you in a generally advantageous negotiating position. This is because the question strongly suggests that you have to run everything by your boss. This is advantageous in that you can easily claim not to have the authority to grant concessions that are asked of you.

The final advantage of "What can you give me that I can take back to my boss?" is where this question moves the focus of the negotiations. It pushes the person you are negotiating with to find ways to meet your needs. This is a very good place for the negotiation to be.

The best time to use "What can you give me that I can take back to my boss?" is when negotiations become deadlocked. Used at this time, the question becomes infinitely more powerful since its use also implies that the negotiations will fail if more concessions are not forthcoming. In such circumstances, it is highly risky for the person you are negotiating with not to come up with additional concessions since he might very well lose the entire deal. This fear of failure is what will push the person you are negotiating with to make the further concession you are seeking.

In order to be best positioned to use this question, it can be a good idea to appoint someone to negotiate who does not have full authority to bind your organization and make concessions. If your negotiator is the boss, and he has no boss of his own, he will not be able to use this question. Sometimes a modified version of this question can be used in such situations, such as "What can you give me that I can take back to my board, employees, team, spouse, partners, etc.?" The idea here is the same: I answer to other people and need something additional to convince the people I am answering to.

One final note. Look carefully at the wording of this question. When negotiating, how you word your questions matters greatly. One of the reasons "What can you give me that I can take back to my boss?" is so effective is because to respond with a simple "nothing" might be harsh and unreasonable. Because of the wording of the question, therefore, you are far more likely to get some type of a concession, even a small one.

We routinely use this question to get better deals. It almost always works. For example, recently we were negotiating a six-figure contract with a potential vendor. One of us was charged with negotiating. The negotiations went back and forth for two weeks. We obtained a number of concessions, but then additional ones were no longer forthcoming, and the negotiation reached a deadlock. At this point the designated negotiator called up the potential vendor. Here's how the negotiation went:

AUTHOR: Jeanne, thank you very much for your proposal and all your hard work. I think it's looking very enticing, but my boss isn't convinced. He's adamant that we should go in another direction. You've never met him; let's just say he's "strong willed."

VENDOR: Wow, we've already given you most of what you asked for. I don't know if we have anything more to give. What's he looking for?

AUTHOR: A further price concession on staff room rate. He is very firm on that since he is high on another vendor that offered a staff rate of $99 a night, whereas you guys are at $150 a night.

VENDOR: Uh-huh.

AUTHOR: What can you give me that I can take back to my boss?

VENDOR: Let me see what I can do.

The next day the vendor called back and offered an additional $5,000 in concessions. Note how we waited to use the "What can you give me that I can take back to my boss?" question until we had already pushed the person we were negotiating with close to her breaking point and were seemingly deadlocked. Bringing the approval of the boss into play, giving specific reasons why the boss was not satisfied, and stressing our alternatives helped gain us a final major concession after the previous deadlock.

We commonly use this question to push our employees to obtain better deals for our firm. Here's how we do it. Let's say we were asking an employee to bid out some work that we needed done. We have trained our employees first to get competitive bids. Next, they have been trained to play each of the vendors off against each other to get lower bids. When we have a low bid we then tell our employee to get us more concessions. When they ask how, we tell them to tell the vendor that their boss wants a better price before he'll agree and to ask "Can you give me something that I can take back to my boss?" We have found that this last technique will often yield additional concessions. An added benefit is that our employees are readily willing to use this technique since they are not being asked to be the bad guy and they can blame things on us.

Lesson

Asking "What can you give me that I can take back to my boss?" will encourage the person you are negotiating with to come up with one last clinching concession. This question is best employed when the negotiation has reached a deadlock. To be able to use this question, it is important to send someone to negotiate who does not have full authority to make concessions and make a deal.

How to Respond If You Are Asked "What can you give me that I can take back to my boss?"

There are three different tacks you can take when responding to this question. First, you can take the bait and offer a small concession that is specifically conditioned on them closing the deal immediately. If you have room to negotiate and can effectively end the haggling, this might be worth it to you, and the person you are dealing with will look like a hero for squeezing another concession out of you. For example, "Well, I've already been pushed pretty hard here. I could check with my boss to see if we could offer a free thirty days if you signed by close of business today." Note here how you protected yourself by stating that your boss would also need to sign off.

Another way to handle this question is to state how you would be more than happy to talk to the other party's boss directly. If this was just a gambit the odds are that the boss has no time and interest to talk to you. The result is an effective parrying of the question. For example, "I'd be happy to talk to your boss directly. I'm available all day if he would like to call." Note that if they take you up on your offer you are still in a better spot since you have conceded nothing but are now dealing with a person with higher authority than your previous point of contact.

A third way to handle this question is to use it as an opportunity to restate the benefits of your service and to put pressure on the other party. The idea here is to launch into another sell job and to try to build power. For example, "You can tell him that you will love our product and that it will save him a lot of time and money, but that our sale ends today so he should decide immediately."

PART IX

Closers

INTRODUCTION: The most difficult part of any negotiation is closing the deal. The other party may hesitate to come to a final agreement because doing so will commit him to the deal. The questions in this section are designed to help you finalize the agreement and close the deal.

Question #41

IF IT'S OKAY WITH YOU THEN, I'LL CALL MY LAWYER AND HAVE HER SEND OVER A CONTRACT?

Five important lessons we have learned over the years are as follows:

1. *Finalizing a negotiation can be difficult.*

2. *The devil is often in the details.*

3. *Lawyers can be torturously slow.*

4. *It is usually to your advantage to have your own lawyer draft an agreement.*

5. *Long, complicated formal contracts can slow down the pace of business and waste a tremendous amount of time.*

"If it's okay with you then, I'll call my lawyer and have her send over a contract?" is a question that is designed to address all of the above problems. Obviously, this question is only appropriate for situations where a formal written contract is needed or expected. It works best in business-to-business negotiations where the party you are negotiating with has flexibility on who will draft the contract—many large organizations require their in-house lawyers to draft contracts or require that a standard form contract be used.

Oftentimes during negotiations, the party you are negotiating with will respond to an offer of yours somewhat equivocally. For example, if you stated, "Well, what if we were to lower the price to $10,000 a month but increase the term to sixteen months?" the answer might come back, "I could live with that" or, "That sounds very tempting" instead of an unequivocal "You've got yourself a deal." The question "If it's okay with you then, I'll call my lawyer and have her send over a contract?" is designed to close out the negotiations by getting the person you are negotiating with to answer "yes" and to stop either equivocating or asking for additional concessions. "If it's okay with you then, I'll call my lawyer and have her send over a contract?" is, therefore, a great question to ask when you would like to push a negotiation to a conclusion.

"If it's okay with you then, I'll call my lawyer and have her send over a contract?" is further designed to give you an advantage by getting the person you are negotiating with to agree that *your* lawyer will draft the initial contract. Having your lawyer draft the initial agreement has numerous advantages. First, lawyers can be very, very slow at producing contracts. You have much more influence over your own lawyer than that of the person you are negotiating with. As such, you have a much better chance of getting a contract quickly from your own lawyer. Since delay often costs money, speeding final execution along can often be a key advantage. In addition, a delay may give the person you are negotiating with an opportunity to change their mind.

The devil in many contracts can often be in the details and legalese. Having your lawyer draft the initial contract will be to your advantage since your lawyer will presumably readily protect your interests in the fine print. The other side's lawyer will, of course, be expected to request changes to the draft contract. You will be in an advantageous position, however, because the starting point for the contractual language negotiations will be contractual language favorable to you, which has been drafted by your own lawyer.

Through our business careers we have seen many verbal deals fall apart, come close to falling apart, or at the very least become unnecessarily delayed when formal written contracts are drafted. The most common reason for this is where one side creates a long, overly complicated and pointlessly overbearing contract. Where your lawyer drafts the contract you can ask the lawyer to keep the contract as simple as possible and to avoid going over the top with one-sided language. Wherever possible the contracts we draft are one page. Keeping written contracts short and simple can be hugely helpful to closing a deal in a reasonable amount of time.

The person you are negotiating with will often readily agree to your lawyer drafting the initial contract since they may be lazy, it will save them legal fees, and they might have been caught off guard and not realized the importance of this concession. Indeed, one of the beautiful features of this question and what makes it very enticing is that you appear to be making a concession by offering to cover the expense and duty of having your own lawyer prepare the contract. Note that the obvious disadvantage of having your lawyer draft the initial contract is that your legal fees will be higher. In many situations, however, the extra legal fees you pay will be well worth executing an advantageous agreement in a timely fashion.

A final advantage of this question is that it is very low risk. "If it's okay with you then, I'll call my lawyer and have her send over a contract?" is a businesslike and nonoffensive question. The worst the person you are negotiating with can say is some form of "no." This will likely be because they don't feel they have reached an agreement with you yet or they cannot agree to your lawyer creating the first draft (usually because they are required by some corporate policy to use a standard form or have their lawyers prepare the initial draft contract).

Consider the following two related examples. Many years ago, we produced a series of educational videotapes for professionals. Part of the deal involving their production was that a certain large nonprofit organization would be the exclusive distributor of the videos. Our agreement was to split the revenue from the videos with the nonprofit 50-50. Since the videos sold for $500 and we were producing many hundreds of copies, there were large amounts of money involved.

After we reached a verbal agreement and shook hands with the executives at the nonprofit, those executives stated that they would have their legal department send over an agreement. We waited and waited. After many weeks and numerous follow-ups of "Where is the contract?" we finally received a draft contract. The contract was many pages too long and very overbearing. It took us several weeks of back-and-forth to negotiate terms we could live with. In the meantime, our time-sensitive video production project was stalled. We were losing money every day that we faced delay. Had we asked "If it's okay with you then, I'll call my lawyer and have her send over a contract?" at the close of negotiations we may very well have ended up with more favorable contractual fine print and could likely have avoided a costly delay.

The video deal with the nonprofit turned out to be a success. A year later, we proposed another video deal with the nonprofit. This time, at the close of the business discussions we asked, "If it's okay with you then, I'll call my lawyer and have her send over a contract?" The nonprofit agreed. Because our lawyer drafted the initial agreement, the deal's fine print was much more favorable to us. Equally or more important, we were able to get a draft contract out to the nonprofit very quickly. The result was a more favorable final contract, executed in a far more timely manner.

Lesson

"If it's okay with you then, I'll call my lawyer and have her send over a contract?" is a low-risk question that can be very helpful in pushing a negotiation to a conclusion. This question can also help you by speeding the execution of the final contract and by making it far more likely that the ultimate fine print in the final contract will protect your interests.

How to Respond If You Are Asked "If it's okay with you then, I'll call my lawyer and have her send over a contract?"

There are several ways to respond to this question. If you are not happy with where things stand (or if you just want to try to get a little better deal) you can certainly use this as an opportunity to request another concession. Since the person you are negotiating with is so eager to do the deal that they're willing to pay the extra legal fees, you might have some good luck gaining a final concession or two. For example, "I don't think we're quite ready for that yet. But if you were to knock another $2,500 off, we could be." If they agree to this final concession you can, of course, still insist that your lawyer draft the contract (for example, and as discussed below, because of corporate policy).

A second way to respond to this question is to offer to have your own lawyer draft the contract. You might even be able to gain another concession. For example, "I'll tell you what, my lawyer is on flat retainer. We'll have my lawyer draft the contract, you'll save $2,000 in legal fees, and we can split the savings by your taking $1,000 off my price. Okay?"

A third way to handle this question is to point to corporate policy. This is a very common response. For example, "I am sorry, when we finalize things and are ready for this we'll need to use our standard contract. It's corporate policy."

A final way to respond to this question is with a simple "yes." This is the best response where you are happy with the deal, wish to close it, are not worried about the contract language, and would like to save money on legal fees. As in most negotiations, the best answer will depend upon your specific situation and goals.

Question #42

CAN WE SET UP A TIME TO FINALIZE THINGS ON [LAST DAY OF THE MONTH]?

Many years ago, we were negotiating a six-figure purchase with a salesperson. The negotiations had been going on for some time with not much favorable movement in our direction. Then we received a call from the salesperson with an ill-advised request: "Is there any way we can wrap this up by the end of the month?" A lightbulb went off in our heads. Obviously, the salesperson's commissions and sales totals or quotas closed at the end of the month. We decided to use this to maximum advantage and replied, "We're tied up the next couple of days, the 28th and 29th; can we set up a time to finalize things on Wednesday the 30th?" When we talked on the 30th, we stiffened our bargaining position. The negotiation went very favorably for us and the salesperson relented on almost all outstanding points. Much more important, we had learned a new negotiating technique and question that we have used successfully for many years since.

As a rule, we now routinely try to schedule closing or final negotiations with commissioned salespersons at the very end of the month, quarter, or year. The easy way to do this is to try to schedule what you hope will be your final negotiation session at the end of the month, quarter, or year by asking, "Can we set up a time to finalize things on [last day of the month]?" We have found salespersons to be much more flexible when they are up against a deadline that determines if they meet their quota or how much money they will be bringing home the following month.

There are obvious limitations to the use of "Can we set up a time to finalize things on [last day of the month]?" This technique is not likely to be of benefit unless you are dealing with a salesperson to whom month-end numbers actually mean something. Buying a used car or lawn mower in a private person-to-person sale is not an appropriate time to use this question.

The best time to use "Can we set up a time to finalize things on [last day of the month]?" is after negotiations have gone on for a while and are stalemated. In this situation, the salesperson will probably understand that concessions will be needed to close the deal. He will be most likely to make those concessions when facing the month-end deadline that has personal ramifications to himself and his family. The implicit message in your question that you are looking to close the deal will also motivate him to do what it takes to get you to say "yes."

Another limitation is that this question will be problematic if you need to close the deal quickly. If your business is being disrupted and you are losing profits each day (say, because a key piece of equipment needs to be replaced) it may not make sense to delay a deal by using this technique. "Can we set up a time to finalize things on [last day of the month]?" obviously will make the most sense when you are under no duress to make your purchase.

"Can we set up a time to finalize things on [last day of the month]?" works best when done in a nonobvious manner. You should never overtly state that you are trying to pressure the salesperson into an end-of-month situation. If you do so, you may seem manipulative and this question could very well backfire.

"Can we set up a time to finalize things on [last day of the month]?" should be routinely used when you are negotiating a major purchase with a professional salesperson. In these situations the question brings with it little risk as long as you can afford to hold off purchasing and don't make what you're really doing obvious. The results you get with the question are often good. Since the risks are minimal and it is often effective, this is a question that should be used routinely.

An almost must-use situation for "Can we set up a time to talk on [last day of the month]?" is where the salesperson explicitly asks that the deal be done before the end of the month, quarter, or year. We have found that this happens more than you would think. Such a verbal leak provides you very valuable insight that the salesperson is motivated to get the deal done by the requested date. Good listening skills are often required to pick up on such leaks, but sometimes they are not. For example, very recently we received an e-mail from a salesperson with whom we were negotiating a five-figure deal. It read in part: "If there is any way we could get this signed up before the end of the month I would be really, really appreciative." In such obvious situations, setting up a final negotiating session for right before the deadline can be very beneficial.

Lesson

One of the most important lessons that can be learned regarding negotiating is that deadlines make things happen. When negotiating with a commissioned salesperson, we learned early on that month-, quarter-, or year-end can be an important deadline that you can use to increase your negotiating advantage. An easy way to use this deadline to your advantage is to ask for a final negotiation session to close the deal at the very end of the month, quarter or year. If this is done in a nonobvious manner, "Can we set up a time to finalize things on [last day of the month]?" is a low-risk way to get a better deal. This question can be especially effective if the salesperson lets slip or requests that a deal be closed by the month's end.

How to Respond If You Are Asked "Can we set up a time to finalize things on [last day of the month]?"

How you best respond to this question is determined by whether or not you are a commissioned salesperson or in another way face an unstated internal month-end deadline. If you don't have such a deadline and want to avoid appearing to be overeager, your answer can be a simple "Sounds good. How about 9:00 A.M.* on the 30th." If you are facing an internal deadline your best response might be just to pick up the phone and try to finalize things right away.

---

* On a related note, one way to impress people when negotiating is with the times you are available to talk. For example, let's say you wanted to impress people with how hard you work or how responsive you are. In this situation, you could say that you are available to talk starting at 5:30 A.M. or 6:00 A.M. or whatever early time you usually make it to your desk. The subtext here is clear—I am a hard-working, productive person.

Question #43

DOES MY PROPOSAL WORK FOR YOU?

As lawyers, the authors were taught from our earliest training that *how* you ask something can matter as much or more than what you ask. We were also taught that if you want to push someone you are cross-examining to the answer you want, use a leading question. Finally, we were taught never to ask an open-ended question during cross-examination because you will then lose all control over the answer that you receive.

Precisely how you ask something can also be extremely important when negotiating. "Does my proposal work for you?" is a polite and gentle way of pushing the recipient to agree to your terms without negotiating at all. In fact, the question is designed to completely avoid any and all negotiating. The answer implicitly requested is either a "yes" or "no" with no negotiating. If the answer does come back that the proposal doesn't work, you have also not painted yourself in a corner as you would have had you stated "Take it or leave it." As such, you have left yourself the option of whether to consider making concessions or explicitly staking out a "take it or leave it" position.

Let's talk some more about what we mean concerning how something is asked. Let's say you were to ask in a negotiation, "What do you think about my proposal?" Now that question on the surface sounds an awful lot like, "Does my proposal work for you?" It isn't. "Does my proposal work for you?" is a close-ended question that invites only a "yes" or "no" response. "What do you think about my proposal?" is an open-ended question that invites open-ended responses such as criticisms, complaints, stories, requests for concessions, and questions. "What do you think about my proposal?" also gives the *impression* of a weakness of your negotiating position since you are telegraphing flexibility and openness to changes in your proposal.

Nobody likes to hear the words "Take it or leave it" during a negotiation. First, hearing these words generally means that you will not be able to gain any additional concessions. Second, the words themselves can be completely offensive by suggesting that the other person is not interested in even hearing anything else that you have to say. "Does my proposal work for you?" is a much gentler and thus more effective way of trying to get the person you are negotiating with to agree without modification to the terms you have suggested. The genius of the question is that while it appears to take into account the other person's desires and concerns, it really does not, since the person you are negotiating with is being pushed into a "yes" or "no" response.

"Does my proposal work for you?" can be particularly effective in situations where you have a vastly superior negotiating position and can use a de facto take-it-or-leave-it strategy. The key to being able to deploy this negotiation question successfully in such a situation is to put yourself in a rock-solid negotiating position. This is done by developing your own alternatives and gathering information. You will likewise be in a superior negotiating position when you can determine that the person you are negotiating with has few alternatives, is operating under a tight deadline, or is desperate to make a deal happen.

You can also use "Does my proposal work for you?" in any situation where you would like to attempt to preempt a long and drawn-out negotiation away from your initial proposal. The beauty of the question in this situation is twofold. First, although you may not have superior negotiating power in the negotiation at hand, *you appear to* by asking such a confident question. Second, the wording of the question is pushing the person you are negotiating with to the simple "yes" response that you are seeking.

The final advantage of "Does my proposal work for you?" is that it is a low-risk question to ask. Before using a question such as "Does my proposal work for you?" you should always consider what the risk is. That is, what will you say if the answer comes back "no" (i.e., "leave it") or if the person you asked the question to makes a counterproposal. A sophisticated negotiator will be prepared to respond to a "no" either by coming back with an explicit stating of "Take it or leave it," or by exploring some give-and-take by asking, "What in particular do you have issue with?" As you can see from the above, a major advantage of "Does my proposal work for you?" is that it also leaves you more flexibility than had you simply stated "Take it or leave it," and is thus far less risky. Furthermore, as described above, the question is not likely to offend the person you direct it to because it is gently worded and even appears to take his or her concerns into consideration.

Let's look at an in-depth example of how the authors have used "Does my proposal work for you?" in a negotiation. Part of our business is to serve as consultants and trainers. We have positioned ourselves in relatively narrow niches such as training expert witnesses how to testify more effectively, showing expert witnesses how to grow their practices, and negotiation consulting. In such a niche market for training and consulting, there is little competition and no customary pricing. As such, every time we are hired to do something there could be endless time consumed with often fruitless negotiations. If we spent too much time negotiating, we would have very little time left to make money, so we very often use "Does my proposal work for you?" as a way to show negotiating power and push the people we are negotiating with to acceptance of our fee structure.

Here's how a recent typical training negotiation went for us.

POTENTIAL CLIENT: Hi, I am the director of training at a Fortune 500 company and would like you to come down to New Orleans on August 15 and train one hundred of our consultants on how to be more effective when testifying.

AUTHORS: How did you hear of us?

POTENTIAL CLIENT: Two of our consultants attended your classes and raved about them.

AUTHORS: How much money do your consultants bill out at?

POTENTIAL CLIENT: $450 to $650 per hour.

AUTHORS: The price is $15,000. That is all-inclusive. It includes handbooks and our travel. Does our proposal work for you?

POTENTIAL CLIENT: Gee, can't you do it for anything less than that?

AUTHORS: We are the most experienced and most effective persons anywhere doing this type of training. I can provide you with numerous letters of reference if you wish. We prepare by reading and reviewing thousands of pages of documentation submitted by your employees so that we can perform extremely realistic mock direct and cross-examinations. We provide an outstanding product and the best we can do on price is $15,000.

POTENTIAL CLIENT: Let me check with my superiors.

Two weeks later they called back and hired us for the $15,000. Our asking "Does our proposal work for you?" helped reinforce our inherent bargaining power, discouraged haggling, and nudged the client into accepting our proposal. The question also helped to push things to a rapid conclusion and greatly reduced the chance of our wasting time in endless negotiations over price.

Let's analyze this example further. First, let's focus on bargaining power. Notice how the questions we asked were designed to increase our bargaining power. The most common way clients find us is through positive word of mouth. That is one reason why we asked how they found us.[1] We were hoping for and received the answer that we came highly recommended. We also asked what their consultants charged to help our position. This was a highly lucrative business unit responsible for hundreds of millions of dollars worth of billable hours each year. This confirmed that they obviously could afford to pay us what we were worth and what we proposed.

Now let's focus on the advantage of using gentle, polite, and professional language where possible. When presenting our proposal we stated, "The price is $15,000. That is all-inclusive. It includes handbooks and our travel. Does our proposal work for you?" It goes without saying that this is a much less offensive, less risky, and much more professional than if we had stated, "The price is $15,000, all-inclusive, take it or leave it." Had we explicitly stated "Take it or leave it," there was a real chance that the potential client would have been so offended that they would not want to do any business with us at any price.

Finally, let's focus on the wiggle room that "Does our proposal work for you?" left us and how it was to our own advantage to not paint ourselves into a corner with a completely inflexible demand. Let's say that the potential client had responded by countering that they would like to arrange to make our training annual but would need a break on our price. Repeat business is something we are obviously very interested in. As such, the flexibility of "Does our proposal work for you?" put us in a position where we could seize such an opportunity:

AUTHORS: The price is $15,000. That is all-inclusive. It includes handbooks and our travel. Does our proposal work for you?

1. Please see Question #1.

POTENTIAL CLIENT: What if we were to make this a multiyear deal where we have you back annually?[2] How much flexibility would you have in your price?[3]

AUTHORS: For an annual deal with a three-year minimum we can do it for $12,500 each year.

POTENTIAL CLIENT: Done.

Lesson

"Does our proposal work for you?" is an extremely well-designed question to use for numerous reasons. First, it is polite and professional and thus not risky. Second, the question nudges the person of whom it is asked to accept your proposal without further negotiating and discourages counterproposals. Third, "Does our proposal work for you?" communicates the helpful perception that you believe you have negotiating power. Finally, "Does our proposal work for you?" leaves you sufficient flexibility in case the person you are negotiating with responds in the negative or with a counterproposal of their own.

How to Respond If You Are Asked "Does my proposal work for you?"

One way to respond to this question is with a simple "no." This can communicate that you believe you have strength in your position and may solicit a response that inquires what you feel is missing in the proposal. The directness of your response may impress the other party with your firmness and confidence. The risk, of course, is that the other party might just walk away.

Another potential response that may help to build your negotiating power is something like, "I am sorry, but we haven't looked it over yet. We are contacting multiple vendors and will get back to

2. Please see Question #25.
3. Please see Question # 26.

you after we have reviewed all proposals." Such a response builds power by showing you are not desperate and are actively courting alternatives.

A third way to respond is to stake out in your responses your own negotiating positions that would ideally leave you some room to negotiate. The idea here is not to directly answer "Does my proposal work for you?" but instead, and in reality, answer the broader question "What do you think of my proposal?" Not exactly answering the question asked is a technique that politicians have mastered. When faced with a question they don't find to their advantage, they just answer the question they would have preferred to have been asked. The thing is, journalists almost never push politicians on this, since dodging in this way is basically accepted. In negotiating, you are also very unlikely to get pushed. With all this said, you could certainly answer with something like, "Here are my thoughts. We have seven main concerns. First, your price is too high. . . ."

PART X

Head Games

INTRODUCTION: Fear, greed, flattery, and un-
certainty can all be used to your advantage in a
negotiation. The questions in this section are
designed to help you utilize overt or subtle psychological pressure to help obtain your negotiating
goals.

Question #44

HOW MUCH TIME, EFFORT, AND MONEY HAVE YOU INVESTED IN YOUR PROPOSAL?

This is a great question to ask when it is obvious that the person you are negotiating with has put a good deal of effort into reaching a deal. The more the person you are negotiating with has expended in time, effort, expenses, emotional energy, and planning, the more invested they are in reaching a negotiated agreement. This increases the power you have in the negotiation. Asking this question at precisely the right time during a negotiation (usually during a deadlock) can reveal several points:

- The person you are negotiating with has really invested too much to come away empty-handed.

- If they do walk away, all the time and money invested will be totally lost and they will have to justify and explain this loss to their colleagues and superiors.

- The person you are negotiating with will likely conduct a cost-benefit analysis to see which will be more expensive—walking away with no agreement or conceding on a few more points than they'd initially planned to in order to achieve a negotiated agreement.

- You, on the other hand, are not heavily invested and are prepared to walk away.

- You appear to feel sorry for the person you are negotiating with for apparently wasting so much time and money, which sends an implicit message that the person you are negotiating with is about to blow the negotiation.

Where the person you are negotiating with appears to be heavily invested in trying to make a deal happen, this question can be extraordinarily effective. Consider a couple of examples from our own experiences.

A few years back, on behalf of a client, we were negotiating a major, long-term publishing contract with a large scientific publishing corporation with offices worldwide. The corporation sent five persons to the negotiation session, which grew intense. These people included:

- Their chief deal maker

- An IT specialist, who was there to explain the technical aspects of their proposal

- The person who had drafted the proposal and who flew in from Germany to answer technical questions

- An attractive sales executive to run through their extensive PowerPoint presentation

- An attractive young woman (playing the role of Vanna White) to flip the pages on a flip chart and to put up specially designed color graphs and charts

It was obvious to us that the company had spent $50,000 to $100,000 or more in time and out-of-pocket expenses to put together all the materials and fly people in from different cities in the United States and Europe. As such, we felt we could get an even better deal than what they had put on the table. When we reached an impasse in the negotiations and wanted them to sweeten their offer we simply said, "It's too bad you might have to go home empty-handed. How much time, effort, and money have you invested in your proposal?"

The reply was very instructive and set the tone for the rest of the negotiation.

"Actually, we have spent a lot of money and time—we are very serious about getting an agreement."

The corporate negotiating team quickly realized that with this major investment, they could walk away from the table only if we pushed well beyond their breaking point. This simple question politely reminded them that we had the power in the negotiation and that they should make their proposal more attractive so they didn't risk losing their entire investment. In fact, soon after this exchange the terms we were offered greatly improved.

Another example. We were negotiating with a software development company to program a piece of software that we were going to bring to market. The software was going to use our proprietary knowledge to help expert witnesses draft better-written reports. The chief executive officer of the software development company and his chief operating officer came out to our offices to pitch their services. Over a period of weeks we worked closely with the company, nailing down the specs of the software that we needed built. During the negotiations they invited us to lunch at a fancy private club they belonged to.

Eventually, after many conversations and much work on the software developer's side, a detailed proposal was e-mailed over to us. Unfortunately, the price was three times what we wanted to pay. We felt that we could get our price from another developer, but we wanted to work with the company we had been negotiating with because of their reputation for quality.

It was at this point that we deployed the "investment" question. We had a conversation with the CEO. We apologized, telling him that we could not afford their services. We complimented them on their work. We told them how impressed we were with them, and then asked, "How much time did you invest trying to make this happen?" The very frustrated CEO blurted out in a fatigued voice, "A lot, and it looks like I just wasted a lot of time and money." We again apologized and wished them the best.

Two days later the CEO called back with a new proposal, which matched our requested price and which was 33 percent of what they were originally going to charge us. Not a bad result for asking one simple question.

Lesson

The question "How much time, effort, and money have you invested in your proposal?" is an excellent question to use to push a heavily invested person into making additional concessions. Don't be afraid to use it with someone who reveals or suggests that they are heavily invested in making a deal happen.

How to Respond If You Are Asked
"How much time, effort, and money
have you invested in your proposal?"

The point of this question is to get you thinking (and freaking out) about what you have to lose if the deal doesn't go through. Accordingly, a good way to answer is not to take the bait. Do not appear at all bothered by the effort you have put in so far. To turn this around you could also politely turn attention back to what the other party has to lose if they don't go through with the deal. For example, "We give the best for our clients. We understand that you stand to [save or lose] a lot of money unless we can get this closed quickly, so we were happy to push to get you our best proposal."

Question #45

WHAT WILL YOU DO IF WE CANNOT REACH AN AGREEMENT?

One advantage to this question is that under *any* circumstances it implies that you are not overeager for an agreement. When you raise the distinct possibility of a deadlock or no negotiated agreement in the end, the person you are negotiating with may logically think that you don't need a deal and will require additional enticements to get you to come to an agreement. The hope, of course, is a better offer and greater concessions.

This is a great question if you want to find out if the person you are negotiating with has any viable alternatives to making an agreement with you. If they do present any viable alternatives, then you're in a more informed bargaining position and can decide how to proceed with the negotiation to your advantage.

If, on the other hand, the person you are negotiating with does not have alternatives, the way this question is phrased ("What will *you* do?") can really be effective for a couple of reasons. First, getting the person you are negotiating with to admit that something unpleasant will happen to him if there is not a deal will increase your leverage in the negotiation. Even if this doesn't happen (it usually doesn't), the idea, of course, is to get the person you are negotiating with to start to think of what happens *to him or her personally* if he or she can't close the deal. This was the job he was sent to do and he did not get the job done. Nobody wants to think of himself (or have others think of him) as a person who cannot or did not get the job done. Nobody wants to disappoint. In this way, the question can be quite effective even if the person you directed it to doesn't answer it at all, since it serves to remind the person you are negotiating with of the potential personal ramifications of their failure to reach an agreement with you.

Let's look at some examples. One of the businesses that we are involved in is setting up seminars and conferences. These are usually held at hotels. A couple of years ago, we were negotiating with a hotel we wanted to move an annual conference to. We were dealing with the sales manager who reports directly to the general manager (i.e., the chief executive) of the hotel. The negotiation was bogged down on price issues so we asked the sales manager what she would do if we didn't reach an agreement. This was a good question since it showed that we weren't overly eager to reach a deal with them (we had also mentioned that we were talking to their competitors as well), that we might get a response that she needed a deal at all costs, or that, at the very least, it would put psychological pressure on her to avoid losing the deal and have to report this failure to her boss, the general manager.

The answer came back that they were also negotiating with a certain medical society for them to use their hotel on the dates we'd asked for the annual conference. We used this information to move the negotiation forward to our benefit. We pointed out that the medical society must change cities every year to satisfy its members whereas we planned to come back to their hotel year after year. We were, therefore, a potentially much more valuable client and deserved superior pricing. The argument worked and they met our price. The negotiation was moved forward because we had asked what the sales manager would do if we couldn't reach an agreement—which would be to make a deal with the medical society who was a far less valuable client than us. The power and utility of asking the right question at the right time during a negotiation should never be underestimated.

In 2008, Jerry Yang of Yahoo was negotiating with Steve Ballmer of Microsoft for the sale of Yahoo. Yang rejected a $45.7 billion offer to sell Yahoo. This failure to reach an agreement may have resulted in as much as a $20 billion loss to Yahoo's shareholders. Mr. Yang tried to blame Microsoft for the failure. This did not fly with Yahoo's shareholders. Shortly after the failed negotiation, Mr. Yang stepped down as Yahoo's CEO. If Mr. Ballmer had asked Mr. Yang what he would do if they couldn't reach an agreement, the pressure on Mr. Yang might have resulted in him rethinking his foolish refusal to sell his company at a premium price.

"What will you do if we cannot reach an agreement?" is a particularly good question to use when you are negotiating with anyone who has to go back and report to a boss, a committee, or a spouse. By raising the specter of failure, you encourage additional concessions. The authors have used this question successfully in such varied circumstances as dealing with insurance adjusters, business-to-business sales reps, and automotive salespeople.

Lesson

The question "What will you do if we cannot reach an agreement?" is very effective because it shows that you're not overeager, it moves the negotiation forward, it may result in a revealing admission from the person you are negotiating with, and it can apply subtle psychological pressure to this person by appealing to their desire to succeed and not to appear to have failed.

How to Respond If You Are Asked "What will you do if we cannot reach an agreement?"

Like most of these final "head games" questions, the key in responding to them is to refuse to take the bait. This particular question has the benefit of being open-ended. A good answer will provide information that will make it appear as though you are in a very good bargaining position. For example, "There are several similar houses for sale in town that we are looking at. We also might just get a lot and build what we want or just continue renting since the real estate market is tanking and prices and rates are both going down. Your house isn't anywhere near everything we were looking for. If we can't get a price that reflects this fact, we'll just pass." The above sample answer is a good one in that it is responsive, it projects negotiating power, and it in no way paints you into a corner.

Question #46

HOW DID IT FEEL TO RECEIVE THAT AWARD?

A simple fact of life is that people are in general more inclined to want to do business with people whom they like. They are also generally more inclined to grant concessions to someone that they like. People are inclined to like people with similar interests or who show interest in their own background and accomplishments. We have found that an effective way to become liked by the person you are negotiating with is to ask them a question that either puts their background or experiences in a favorable light, somehow shows interests in their accomplishments, or determines that you share similar interests.

The key to making this technique work is to try to determine the X Factor of the person you are negotiating with. The X Factor is what makes the person tick. There can be many clues to what a person's X Factor is. These clues can be found by techniques such as searching the Internet, listening carefully to what the person says, and looking around at what the person has on his résumé or even on the walls of his office.

Once you find the X Factor you can ask a question or series of

questions designed to build rapport with the person you are negotiating with. This is usually best done preemptively, before terms
are discussed. Another good time to use this technique is during a
social or lunch break. Let's look at two examples where we have
used this technique to our advantage.

We were negotiating our first contract with one of the largest scientific organizations in the United States. We traveled to Washington,
D.C., got the guided tour, and then started negotiating. It became
apparent early on that the negotiation was not going well. We were
selling, but they were not buying. Each time a little progress was
made, different hurdles were raised by the organization. For example: "Why should we work with your little company?" "Is your
company large enough to handle this project?" "Do you have
enough redundancy built into your corporate structure?" On and
on the negotiation went, with little progress and no favorable momentum. Around noon the lead negotiator said, "The least we could
do in light of the distance you traveled to get here is to take you out
to lunch." You did not have to be a superb active listener to hear the
implicit message—lunch but no deal.

We broke for lunch and there we asked the lead negotiator,
"How did it feel to get the Medal of Freedom?" We had done some
research and found this bit of information online. The recipient of
the question smiled and talked at length about how proud he was.
He described the awards ceremony in detail. We talked about how
before he was the executive director he was an important scientist.
This is, in fact, what he was proudest of. It was his X Factor. The
tone of the negotiation was abruptly changed from "Why should
we do this with you?" to "How can we get this done?" It was a very
dramatic and abrupt change of attitude.

After lunch, we went back to the office and quickly negotiated
an agreement. There is absolutely no question in our minds that
but for the question "How did it feel to get the Medal of Freedom

from Colin Powell?" we would not have walked out with an agreement. Not only did we stroke his ego, but we were able to show how diligent we are in research and preparation.

A second example. For many years we had been trying to form a business relationship with a very well established national organization. We would send letters and proposals. On good days we would get a polite "no." Most of the time they wouldn't answer at all. Our contact at the company was Jewish. One of the authors (who is Jewish) was able to get our contact on the phone one day and used a Yiddish phrase as a trial balloon. Our contact responded in Yiddish. He then asked, "How often do you go to Israel?" It turns out that we had found an X Factor. Our contact was heavily involved in supporting Israel. She raised money for Israel and even volunteered yearly in the Israeli military. For months we spoke socially about Israel, about the author's trips, our Jewish heritage, our Jewish families, our Jewish upbringing, and so on. We would send her greetings during the Jewish holidays. Once the bond had been well established we asked for and received an in-person meeting to pitch the CEO of the organization. Our contact was now a strong ally and not only did we get a meeting, at the meeting we closed a mutually beneficial long-term deal. Without building such a rapport there is no way we would have been able to close this deal.

This bonding technique has also been used against us to very good effect. One of the nice things about being your own boss is that we try only to deal with people we like. There is an intangible pleasure in dealing with nice people that we have bonded with. It makes transactions more fun and satisfying. You should not underestimate the power of this feeling and how it can influence negotiations.

Recently, one of the authors hired an arborist to do some work

cutting down some trees. The arborist showed up in desert camou-
flage pants, had short hair, and kept calling the author "sir."

"Were you in the military?" the author asked.

"Yes," came back the reply.

"Were you in Iraq?"

"Yes, in 1991 and 2003," came the reply.

"What outfit?"

"82nd Airborne." The arborist had tapped one of the author's X
Factors since the author's father had been in the military for many
years and the author gives money to the USO and other organizations that support the military. The arborist did a very good job
and was paid more than what was agreed upon for a price. When
additional work became needed, it was not bid out. The bottom line
is that tapping the X Factor, even that of a sophisticated negotiator,
can be quite powerful.

Here's another example of this technique being used against us. One
of the authors was negotiating with a salesperson recently for a five-
figure deal. The salesperson went online and saw that we were based
on Cape Cod. Before we started formally negotiating terms she asked,
"Do you live on the Cape?" The answer, of course, was "yes." She then
went on to explain how much she loved the cape and how her family
rented a home in a certain part of the cape every year. The intent was
clear: get us to like her and bond with her so we'd want to do business with her. It worked. We closed that deal and many more since.

Lesson

You will get more and better deals if you build a bond and personal
rapport with the person you are negotiating with. One simple way
to do this is to ask questions designed to put their background or
experiences in a favorable light, somehow show interest in their accomplishments, or determine that you share similar interests.

How to Respond If You Are Asked
"How did it feel to receive that award?"

This appears to be a softball question. The intent, of course, is to suck up to you, befriend you, help you lose your objectivity, and possibly prompt some type of damaging information leak. The best way to resist this tactic is to answer the question narrowly and immediately move the focus back to the negotiation at hand. In effect, you want to be polite but make it perfectly clear that you are all business. For example, "It was quite a privilege. Thank you. Now, another question about your redundancy. What contingency plans do you have for continuity in the event of disability or death?"

Question #47

HAVE YOU CONSIDERED WHAT YOU STAND TO LOSE IF YOU DON'T?

A powerful way to break deadlock and get what you want is to point out what the person you are negotiating with has to lose if he doesn't come to your terms. An easy way to do this is to ask, "Have you considered what you stand to lose if you don't?" The subtext of the question is simple: Don't blow it. Without this deal, you could be in real trouble. Note that this question differs from Question #45 in that the focus is not so much on wasted time and money in negotiating, but on the direct negative consequences of not reaching a deal in terms of paying more somewhere else, not saving the money you could have, etc.

Fear is one of the two emotions that can move prices wildly on the stock market (the other being greed). Fear can also be an extremely influential emotion in a negotiation. "Have you considered what you stand to lose if you don't?" is designed to tap into the fear of failure or loss of the person you are negotiating with. Just as in the stock market, if you can successfully make this person feel fear, you can often achieve very rapid movements in his position.

There are two likely responses to "Have you considered what you stand to lose if you don't?" Both are to your advantage. The first likely response is that the person you are negotiating with will ignore or dodge the question or try to change the subject. For example:

PARTY 1: Have you considered what you stand to lose if you don't?

PARTY 2 (IGNORING THE QUESTION): Let me ask you this, what is your time frame?

If the person you are negotiating with dodges the question similar to the above that's okay. Simply by asking the question you have planted a seed of free-floating anxiety and fear of failure in the person's head. You also may be able to ask "Have you considered what you stand to lose if you don't?" again later on during the negotiation.

The second likely response you will get to "Have you considered what you stand to lose if you don't?" is something to the effect of "What do you mean?" This gives you a tremendous opening to try to put fear into the person you are negotiating with. In order to make the best use of "Have you considered what you stand to lose if you don't?" you need to be ready to powerfully articulate the ills, embarrassments, and lost opportunities that may befall the person you are negotiating with if they don't come around to your position. This requires preparation. In advance of deploying "Have you considered what you stand to lose if you don't?" you should think about the arguments you will make if you are given the opportunity to do so.

"Have you considered what you stand to lose if you don't?" works in almost all types of negotiating, including both buying and selling. It is most appropriately used when deadlock has been reached or the person you are negotiating with needs one final push to get them to agree. The question itself is fairly low risk as long as it is not used prematurely. Beware that if you do use this question too early in a negotiation (before there is a deadlock), it may come off as a high-handed pressure gambit that will turn off the person you are negotiating with.

We have used "Have you considered what you stand to lose if you don't?" repeatedly and successfully over the years. Please consider the following two examples.

Very recently, one of us received a call from a potential client. He was an expert witness who had purchased some of our books on expert witnessing. He had some questions for me about his expert witness practice, which he wanted to grow and make much more profitable. From what he told me in our short conversation I knew that he was making many serious mistakes in his expert witness practice and that he would greatly benefit from attending our annual national conference and preconference on expert witnessing. Here's about how the conversation went:

CLIENT: How long is the conference?
AUTHOR: Four days.
CLIENT: How much does it cost?
AUTHOR: Tuition is $2,000. It's in Chicago at a very reasonably priced hotel with a free airport shuttle, so your total expense will be around $3,000, including tuition, lodging, meals, and airfare.
CLIENT: Wow, that's really expensive.
AUTHOR: Didn't you just ask me if you should go to law school to help be a better expert witness? Between tuition and three years of giving up your practice to go to law school this would cost you more than $300,000. Unlike law school, our program actually teaches you practical things you can and will immediately use.
CLIENT (VOICE WHINY): Your course is $500 a day. It's just very pricey.

AUTHOR: Have you considered what you stand to lose if you don't?

CLIENT (VOICE HESITANT AND NERVOUS): What do you mean?

AUTHOR: Expert witnessing is a one-strike-and-you're-out proposition. If you make one big mistake the word will get out and you will never be hired again. Game over. You will make one of those mistakes soon if you don't get our training. I can almost guarantee it. You mentioned to me almost bombing at a deposition because the lawyer who hired you refused to prepare you. We'll teach you a foolproof way to avoid this problem. You also mentioned your rates. You're not charging enough. We'll show you how to charge substantially more for doing the same work, without pricing yourself out of the market. We'll teach you how to get substantially more business and avoid getting stiffed. The list goes on. This is your career. It's not the time to be penny–wise and pound-foolish.

CLIENT: I get your point. I can't afford *not* to go. Give me the dates of the conference again so that I can block them out on my calendar.

Notice here how we were very well prepared to tell him in powerful and memorable language what he would be losing if he didn't take our deal. In order to use "Have you considered what you stand to lose if you don't?" you need to be well prepared to drive home the specific dire consequences that will come to be if your deal is not taken. If you are well prepared, you will often be able to achieve the same dramatic results we were able to.

Here's another example of where we've used this question to dramatic effect. Recently, we were negotiating to rent some space for a conference we were putting on. Because of somewhat unusual circumstances we needed the space only about six weeks out. This is considered very last-minute in the meeting industry. As with many things last-minute, we saw an opportunity to get a very good deal since the conference center presumably wouldn't want the space to go empty and would be unlikely to get another group to book the space at such a late date.

The normal pricing of the conference center was $94 per person per day. We told them we couldn't pay a dime more than $79. They countered with $85 and there we became deadlocked. We stayed deadlocked through three additional negotiating sessions. We had an alternative site lined up as a backup just in case, so we decided to make one last push to get our price. Here's about how the discussion went:

AUTHOR: Is $85 the best that you can do?

CONFERENCE CENTER: That's a great value for you. Our conference center is top-notch.

AUTHOR: That's too bad, our maximum budget is $79.

CONFERENCE CENTER: Yes, I agree. Your attendees are going to be disappointed with not being at a location as nice as ours.

AUTHOR: Have you considered what you stand to lose if you don't meet our budget?

CONFERENCE CENTER: Nothing. There is another group interested in Saturday.

AUTHOR: Well, I'm sure you've considered that our group is for two days, Saturday and Sunday, and would generate twice as much revenue. From what you've told us in our discussions, you have so much space that you should be able to accommodate both us and the other group as well. It would have been nice to work with you. The last facility we used in your area we came back to for three years in a row. We really like getting comfortable with a place and continuing to use them. The only reason we can't use them this time around is because they are booked. It surprises me that you can't accommodate our budget and are going to let the space lie vacant.

The chances of you getting another group interested at this late date are practically nil, you have the space for us, and we'd be great long-term, repeat business.

CONFERENCE CENTER: I'll call you back within the hour.

About twenty minutes later we got a call from the conference center agreeing to our price. They had completely caved in to our position. Asking "Have you considered what you stand to lose if you don't meet our budget?" broke a seemingly intractable deadlock to our total advantage.

Lesson

An effective way to break deadlock or clinch a deal is to ask "Have you considered what you stand to lose if you don't?" This question will tap into the fears of the person you are negotiating with. At a minimum, "Have you considered what you stand to lose if you don't?" will get the person thinking in the back of his mind about failure. Oftentimes, however, this question will serve as a powerful opening for you to unleash a well-prepared parade of horrors that will befall the person you are negotiating with. Once these potential negatives are considered, you will often be able to move this person dramatically off his or her previous positions. This question should not be used prematurely lest it give the impression of a high-pressure sales tactic that could be a turnoff.

How to Respond If You Are Asked "Have you considered what you stand to lose if you don't?"

This question is designed to get you to show fear. Fear in a negotiation translates to weakness, which will result in subpar results. The key to dealing with this question effectively is an absolute refusal to show any fear. Your response should be confident, and, if possible, also provide gratuitous information that strengthens your bargaining position. For example, "I see you like direct questions. Here's a direct answer. The answer to your question is nothing. I'll just find a better way to do it that doesn't cost as much." Or, "I've got three other potential buyers lined up, so the answer to your question is nothing." Or finally, "Well, I've achieved a fair amount of success without your service, so I'm quite confident I'll be just fine."

An additional way to respond to this question is to push back aggressively by asking the other party to guarantee the pie-in-the-sky results they are claiming you will have.* In effect, you are calling the other party's bluff. For example, "I see you say that I'll be able to double my profits if I buy your machine and that if I don't buy it I'll be out of luck. I assume you're willing to put that in writing and guarantee my doubling of profits?" You are very unlikely to get the guarantee. If you do and it's enforceable, you've won a victory. If you don't get the guarantee, you have at least successfully parried the question and improved your negotiating position by showing skepticism and not fear.

* See also Question #29.

Question #48

WHY SHOULD I CONTINUE TO NEGOTIATE WITH YOU AFTER THAT REMARK?

"Why should I continue to negotiate with you after that remark?" is a situational question. It is designed to be used in the rare circumstances when, during the heat of negotiation, the person you are negotiating with makes a totally inappropriate remark or comment. The remark may be sexist, racist, ethnic, about your sexual orientation, appearance, etc. "Why should I continue to negotiate with you after that remark?" is designed to call the person you are negotiating with on his inappropriate remark and make him pay the price for it.

When used under the proper circumstances, this question can have an immediate and dramatic effect on the negotiation. Once you ask "Why should I continue to negotiate with you after that remark?" the person you are negotiating with will immediately realize that he has made a serious mistake. This mistake could have serious and long-term effects on his career and reputation. At all costs, the person you are negotiating with will want to resolve the situation and put his mistake behind him with his reputation intact.

The subtext of the question is that this was a very serious mistake and that either the person you are negotiating with makes this right or he will pay the consequences. With the above in mind, the person you are negotiating with will almost always apologize profusely and say he didn't mean what he said. Most important, he will likely do whatever it will take to make it right and keep the whole situation quiet.

When you have been insulted in this fashion we suggest that you do not overtly threaten to expose the person you are negotiating with. This may feel good, but is counterproductive if you still want to close a deal as quickly and advantageously as possible. There is also no need to do this as this person is well aware of the potential personal and professional consequences of his gaffe. Taking the high road, accepting a sincere apology, and moving right back to the negotiation is the most effective way to handle this unfortunate situation. The person you are negotiating with will now be very careful about what he says. More important, he will likely be very eager to please you, complete the negotiation to your satisfaction, and sweep the whole matter under the rug.

Every once in awhile, an unfortunate situation arises where we have used this question to great effect. For example, many years ago, one of us was negotiating with a representative from a large national corporation. In the midst of the negotiation, the person I was negotiating with was complaining about the length of the process and my insistence on a better price. In the heat of the negotiation he asked me how much longer I was going to "Jew him down."

The minute the remark came out I tensed up. I took a deep breath, looked him in the eye, and asked, "Why should I keep negotiating with you after an anti-Semitic remark like that?" The instant he heard my question it looked as though he had seen a ghost. He realized the amount of trouble both he and his employer could be in. He immediately apologized for his insensitive remark. I accepted his apology and agreed to continue the negotiation. He was now very agreeable and eager to please. In fact, he was almost docile. Needless to say, the terms I was able to negotiate were extremely favorable.

Here's another quick example. Many years ago, one of the authors and his wife went shopping for a new car. We went into the showroom and the salesperson greeted us. Unfortunately, this was the last communication he made with my wife. Every time my wife asked a question he would direct his answer to me, and not both of us. He asked me a number of questions as to what I wanted, but never asked my wife. He obviously assumed that I was the decision maker. I could see that my wife was about to blow a gasket.

We went into his office to discuss numbers. He asked what we were looking for, meaning a price point. I took a deep breath, looked him in the eye, and replied, "I'm looking for a little respect for my wife. You've been ignoring her and only talking to me. Why should we even continue to discuss a purchase with you?"

The salesman almost turned white. You really can't imagine the look on his face. He offered a very sincere apology. After this incident we kept talking about the car. We received a very favorable price and exceedingly responsive and accommodating service.

If you look at the two examples above you can see the choices you are faced with when you are subject to inappropriate behavior in a negotiation. One way to proceed is to report the offender and walk out. The problem with this approach is that it will not be productive in terms of getting you the deal you are looking for. We instead suggest calling the person on his inappropriate conduct and then using the leverage to drive a harder bargain.

Lesson

There will be times when the person you are negotiating with makes a completely insulting or inappropriate remark. In this situation, asking "Why should I continue to negotiate with you after that remark?" can result in your gaining a powerful advantage in the negotiation. The typical result after you ask this question is an immediate apology. More important, the person you are negotiating with will likely be extremely accommodating and will want to do whatever necessary to make you happy and keep what happened quiet.

How to Respond If You Are Asked "Why should I continue to negotiate with you after that remark?"

This is obviously a tough one. The best way to deal with this question is to prevent it by never making an inappropriate remark. If you really did make a remark that is sexist, racist, ethnic, about someone's sexual orientation, or otherwise clearly offensive and inappropriate,* you are in a very, very difficult position. The best you can do in this situation is to apologize sincerely and hope you are not reported to anyone. You will also, of course, want to learn your lesson and make sure you never repeat this mistake in the future.

---

* Such as a negative comment regarding someone's weight or appearance.

Question #49

WHAT'S IN IT FOR ME?

This direct question is very effective during negotiation because it usually catches the recipient off guard. An off-guard recipient is more likely to leak valuable information.[1] The recipient's natural reaction to the question is to start to "sell" their project or idea. What follows from the recipient usually is a series of reasons to take on the project, its monetary benefits, and its ancillary benefits

The question also suggests a lack of motivation on the part of the person that asks it. This helps the asker of the question gain power in the negotiation and induces the recipient to become defensive. The result is that the person you are negotiating with frequently throws benefits into the mix that he'd not initially planned to offer.

There are several reasons for this. The question implies that the questioner will not take on the project unless there are substantially good reasons to do so. For a lot of people, just asking this question is a significant negotiating step in the right direction. The

1. For more on cleverly gathering information, please see Part I.

question also drives home the point that unless the cost-benefit analysis makes it feasible to conclude the deal, the questioner will not be inclined to take on the project. This is a great question to use when you are "ambushed" by someone calling you out of the blue who starts negotiating with you when you are not prepared to do so.

An ambush negotiation can be effective against you because it catches you off guard and gives you no time to think. In addition, the person ambushing you can quickly gauge by your immediate reaction how excited you are to be asked. The quicker you agree, the less remuneration and benefits he will need to offer you to gain your agreement. When ambushed with a negotiation or a proposal that you were not expecting, asking "What's in it for me?" can immediately defeat the ambush, gather immediate concessions, and help you gain power in the negotiation.

The psychology of "What's in it for me?" is very powerful. The question reminds the person who is trying to get you to do something that unless there are good enough reasons to take on the project, you may very well be better off politely declining the offer. This question also forces the recipient to reveal details about the project that can intentionally be easily glossed over by an experienced negotiator trying to sell the project. Finally, "What's in it for me?" will give the questioner an opportunity to think, and also the chance for you to just say "no," after hearing the response.

Here are some examples of where we've used this to save us time, prioritize our attention, and negotiate better opportunities.

Many years ago, we were approached by a large privately held business that wanted to buy our company. We were flattered by this and were very excited. We negotiated confidentiality agreements, disclosed all kinds of information, and held countless meetings with the prospective buyer. In sum, we spent a lot of time on this and we were very distracted by the process to the degree that we were not spending as much time as we should have running our business. In the end, we received an offer under which we were to give up our control and ownership of our profitable family business in exchange for illiquid shares in the larger business. In effect, they were asking us to invest in them! We, of course, turned down this unfavorable offer, but we had lost a tremendous amount of time and money by being distracted by the whole process.

We learned from this experience. Now, whenever we are approached to sell our business (almost always an ambush, since we are not shopping the business) we ask up front what's in it for us (cash or something other than cash), how much as a multiple of earning the buyer has ever paid for a business,[2] and how much cash the potential buyer has access to. This simple approach has saved us hundreds and hundreds of hours and hence saved us hundreds of thousands of dollars.

We are also accomplished public speakers. We are often asked to give presentations at association meetings across the country. Unfortunately, many organizations pay only nominal or no fees for speaking. Our stature plus the time involved in traveling to give a presentation demands that we be well paid. As a rule, therefore, we ask the question, "What's in it for me?" when we are asked to present. Asking this question quickly and efficiently separates the well-paying offers from the poor-paying ones. Asking this question also tends to induce the person inviting us to make a higher offer since we are clearly indicating that we are not overeager.

When you are looking to buy something, a variation of this question is almost always a good idea. Asking such a question gives you time to think, shows that you are not overeager, and forces the seller to come up with compelling reasons why you should fork over your hard-earned money. Here's an example: Jim and his wife, Nancy, test-drove a luxury car a few years ago, and were deciding

---

2. Please see Question #13.

between a luxury sedan and a less upscale model. We asked the salesman, "Why should we spend the extra money on this, why not get the less upscale model—what's in it for us?" His answer was shocking in its arrogance and ignorance: "This is for a different class of people and I don't sell that less upscale model." This response immediately soured us and provided us with the insight to avoid getting involved with a person like this. We eventually bought the luxury model from someone else, who was able to clearly and politely articulate the value of the model, so that we felt sure about our purchase.

Lesson

"What's in it for me?" can and will save you time and money. Whenever you are asked to do or to purchase something, consider using this question. This question quickly and efficiently separates good offers from poor ones, communicates that you are not over-eager, and helps encourage the recipient to improve their offer.

How to Respond If You Are Asked "What's in it for me?"

Success in negotiation often depends much on how well you are prepared. In order to answer this question most effectively you will need to be well prepared to state, in powerful and understandable terms, the specific benefits of your proposal. For example, "You'll get twice as many channels at a lower price *and* get free phone service." Having a list of reasons well prepared in advance will help you answer the question completely and with confidence.

Question #50

IS THERE ANYTHING ELSE YOU ARE AWARE OF THAT MAY HAVE AN IMPACT ON OUR AGREEMENT OR LONG-TERM RELATIONSHIP?

Oftentimes, the most favorable result you can reach in a negotiation is *not* reaching any agreement at all. This is no time truer than when you are negotiating a potential long-term relationship with an unknown or unreliable party. It is generally not a good idea to get involved on a long-term basis with a party you do not trust. Asking, "Is there anything else you are aware of that may have an impact on our agreement or long-term relationship?" provides you with the opportunity to observe how the person you are negotiating with responds. Any signs of dishonesty or evasiveness should raise red flags.

Another advantage to this question is that the premise of the question strengthens your bargaining position. The premise, of course, is that your relationship will be long-term. As such, this is likely to be a very valuable chunk of business for the person you are negotiating with, and commensurate concessions should logically be in order.

Finally, unlike the split-the-difference question,* this is not a common negotiating question that the person you are negotiating with is prepared for and will be anticipating. Asking "Is there anything else you are aware of that may have an impact on our agreement or long-term relationship?" is likely to catch the person you are negotiating with off guard. Much can then be gleaned from his response and how it is delivered.

A particularly good time to ask this question is when you know something about the party you are negotiating with that that party does not know you know. As we stated above, asking, "Is there anything else you are aware of that may have an impact on our agreement or long-term relationship?" in this situation can allow you to quickly determine if you are dealing with an honorable and trustworthy future partner. When you ask the question, closely observe how the other party responds. A less-than-honest full disclosure may call into question whether you should be doing business with these people at all.

We've used this question to great effect in our own business. A few years ago, we were negotiating another long-term contract with one of the hotels we deal with. The hotel was a bit run-down and our contract was based on the hotel's verbal commitment to undergo renovations. We found out through networking that the hotel was for sale. This was never mentioned to us during the negotiations and we wanted to make sure we were dealing with a trustworthy partner so we set up a meeting with the hotel's general manager. At that meeting, we asked the pointed question, "Is there anything else you are aware of that may have an impact on our agreement or long-term relationship?" The response came back: "Yes, but I need you to hold this in confidence because this is not public information. The hotel is for sale, but part of the terms of the sale is that the renovations need to be completed before your programs." This answer gave us a very solid assurance

* Please see Question #33.

that we were dealing with an honorable person. We closed the deal and have been doing business there ever since—to mutual advantage.

Consider a second example from our experiences. A few years back we were negotiating a long-term distribution contract for some of our training videos that we sell. We didn't get a warm and fuzzy feeling from the person we were negotiating with. We decided to use the "Is there anything else you are aware of that may have an impact on our agreement or long-term relationship?" question to see how the potential distributor would react. The conversation went something like this:

> **AUTHORS:** Is there anything else you are aware of that may have an impact on our agreement or long-term relationship?
> **DISTRIBUTOR:** I really don't know how to answer a question like this. Why raise this now after weeks of negotiating? I thought we were close to an agreement.
> **AUTHORS:** We are, or were.
> **DISTRIBUTOR:** Shouldn't we leave this to the lawyers to deal with stuff like this? They'll put all kinds of standard disclosure language into the agreement.
> **AUTHORS:** We are not considering entering into a long-term relationship with your lawyers; we were considering entering into one with you and your company.
> **DISTRIBUTOR:** Well, much of what you are asking for is proprietary, but I can assure you . . .
> **AUTHORS:** So you either can't or will not answer the question?

We didn't like how this exchange went, so we walked away from the deal. This potentially saved us a lot of money, since it's not a good idea to get into business with people you don't trust.

Consider one final example. The authors were negotiating with an international publishing company over the rights to publish a prestigious journal. Near the conclusion of the negotiation, the author asked the lead negotiator for the publishing company, "Is there anything else you are aware of that may have an impact on our agreement or long-term relationship?" The negotiator conferred with his team and then informed us that they were purchasing another journal in the same field. He went on to explain how and why this would be a positive development for both of us. The negotiator's candor helped cement our trust and relationship, and was one of the reasons we chose to sign with that publisher.

Lesson

Before any negotiation of a long-term contract is completed, you may want to ask the question "Is there anything else you are aware of that may have an impact on our agreement or long-term relationship?" Watch the face of the recipient carefully. Just as in poker, facial expressions and other nonverbal behavior can be revealing. How the recipient goes about answering the question may tell you whether you want to be in business with him and/or with his company. This question can be particularly effective if you know something about the party you are negotiating with that that party doesn't know you know.

How to Respond If You Are Asked "Is there anything else you are aware of that may have an impact on our agreement or long-term relationship?"

First of all, a poker face is in order. It doesn't matter what you say if you look guilty or evasive when saying it. Any signs of guilt or evasion may sink the deal. If there is nothing to disclose, say so and say so directly. For example, "No." If there is something to disclose, disclose it. Failure to do so could result in a breach of trust that will sink the deal. In addition, your candor can help seal the deal since it will build the trust that is an essential ingredient of successful long-term relationships. For example, "Yes. I have cancer. I am in remission and the prognosis is excellent, but you never know. We have a succession plan and my partners will be very able to take excellent care of you if I am unable to. I would also appreciate it if you keep this confidential."

CONCLUSION

We've spent decades practicing, developing, and refining the questions in this book. We've made many negotiating mistakes and have gained many insights into this fascinating and challenging process. We've also taught many courses on negotiating. We always find it helpful at the end of our courses to try to give some final advice on how to connect the dots, so to speak, and to make the most of what we have tried to teach. With that in mind, here are some general guidelines that we hope will make your use of our questions even more effective.

Practice. Negotiating is an art. The more you practice negotiating, the better you will become at negotiating. A good way to practice is to negotiate where the stakes are not that high, such as in a retail situation.

Prepare. Success in negotiations is often much more a result of perspiration than inspiration. Do your homework. Line up alternatives. Gather as much information as possible. Think, in advance, of which of our fifty questions you might use and prepare for the likely responses from the other party.

Develop as much negotiating power and leverage as you can. Shop around. Find alternatives. Don't appear overeager. Don't wait until the last minute. Dangle the potential of a long-term relationship in front of the other party. See Part V.

Obtain and control information. Be careful not to leak to the other party information that can be used against you. Purposefully leak information that strengthens your bargaining position. Gather as much information as you can. See Part I.

You don't have to do what the other party wants you to do. Just because the other party asks you a question to lead you down a certain road does not mean that you need to follow along passively to the slaughter. Avoid the question or answer a question of your own choosing. This happens all the time and you likely won't be called on it.

Start off strong. Consider using some of the Opening Moves of Part III.

Anchor the other party. This insidious technique will force the other party to negotiate back from your opening position. This is described in Part IV.

Deal with the person of highest authority that you can. Such a person will more likely be willing and able to grant you concessions. See Part II.

Recognize that the other party doesn't need to lose for you to win. A win-win solution is oftentimes both the most satisfying *and* is in your best interest. See Part VI.

Do not be afraid of deadlock. Deadlock can be broken without caving in. See Part VIII.

Listen very carefully and observe the other party's expressions. You will usually be best off with your eyes and ears open and your mouth closed.

Don't wait until the last minute. If you are under a deadline you will lose power. Conversely, use the other party's deadlines against them.

Use to your advantage the other party's fear, greed, and vanity. See Part X.

When negotiating price, also consider how the terms of payment can gain you additional concessions. See Part VII.

Finally, we would like you to consider what we believe to be the dirty little secret regarding negotiating. Negotiating *can actually be fun.* It can be quite satisfying to negotiate a good deal. It can also be fun and interesting to practice and improve your negotiating skills and try out the questions in this book.

There is no question in our minds that negotiating skills will make you more successful in business and in life. The question (and answer) format in this book has been designed to make improving your negotiating skills quick, easy, and, yes, actually fun. We sincerely hope that that you are able to use our questions to great effect for the benefit of yourself, your organization, and your family.